THE BEST
Vail Valley
HIKES

THE GORE RANGE GROUP
of
THE COLORADO MOUNTAIN CLUB
with
NATHAN FREE

The Colorado Mountain Club Press
Golden, Colorado

PUBLISHED BY

The Colorado Mountain Club Press
710 Tenth Street, Suite 200, Golden, Colorado 80401
303-996-2743   e-mail: cmcpress@cmc.org

Founded in 1912, The Colorado Mountain Club is the largest outdoor recreation, education, and conservation organization in the Rocky Mountains. Look for our books at your local bookstore or outdoor retailer or online at www.cmc.org/books.

Erika Arroyo: design, composition, and production
Eduard B. Avis: copy editor
John Gascoyne: series editor
Nathan Free: project manager
Christian Green: publisher

CONTACTING THE PUBLISHER

We would appreciate it if readers would alert us to any errors or outdated information by contacting us at the address above.

DISTRIBUTED TO THE BOOK TRADE BY

Mountaineers Books, 1001 SW Klickitat Way, Suite 201, Seattle, WA 98134, 800-553-4453, www.mountaineersbooks.org

TOPOGRAPHIC MAPS are copyright 2009 and were created using National Geographic TOPO! Outdoor Recreation software (www.natgeomaps.com; 800-962-1643).

COVER PHOTO: View looking east from the Upper Piney River Trail. Photo by Dave Cooper

We gratefully acknowledge the financial support of the people of Colorado through the Scientific and Cultural Facilities District of greater Denver for our publishing activities.

WARNING: Although there has been an effort to make the trail descriptions in this book as accurate as possible, some discrepancies may exist between the text and the trails in the field. Hiking in mountainous areas—and canyons and deserts as well—is a high-risk activity. This guidebook is not a substitute for your experience and common sense. The users of this guidebook assume full responsibility for their own safety. Weather, terrain conditions, and individual abilities must be considered before undertaking any of the hikes in this guide.

First Edition

ISBN 978-0-9842213-6-3

Printed in China

I dedicate this book to a wonderful woman who has "moved on" to that big mountain in the sky—Jean McGuey.

Jean was one of the founders of our local chapter of the Colorado Mountain Club, the Gore Range Group, and first introduced me to the CMC in 1991. At the time, she was a fellow ski instructor and very passionate about the outdoors. She furthered the mission of the CMC through all types of activities, while promoting education and preservation of our environment.

Always the explorer, and quick to identify flora and fauna along the way, Jean was an avid mountaineer and proud "summiter" of Colorado's Top 100 Peaks—all over 13,800 feet. But most important to our local organization, she was a cheerleader for "the Club", as we called it—an organizer and a motivator for others to participate fully. She was, in every way, a great person.

I realized later on, after Jean's passing, that one of the biggest things that drew me to love and appreciate her was how she espoused so many traits that my mother offered in my childhood, including an incredible drive to accomplish most anything—regardless of how formidable—and without panic, all while holding onto a gentle love of nature along the way.

Now, I often feel Jean's presence in the stillness of the quiet outdoors; although she has gone around a corner in the trail and is no longer visible, I know she is still there.

—*Nathan Free*

(See the "End of the Trail" tribute to Jean in *Trail and Timberline*, Spring 2005, by Allen Best.)

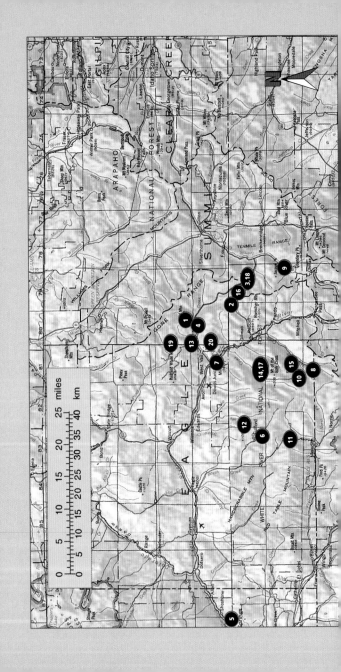

CONTENTS

Acknowledgments 6
Foreword 7

Introduction 9
The Ten Essentials Systems 12
Camping and Backpacking Information 17

THE HIKES
1 Booth Creek Trail 20
2 Bowman's Shortcut to Top of the World 24
3 Corral Creek 28
4 Gore Valley Trail 32
5 Grizzly Creek 36
6 Lake Charles/Mystic Island Lake 40
7 Lionshead Rock 44
8 Lonesome Lake 48
9 Mayflower Gulch 52
10 Missouri Pass/Fancy Pass 56
11 Mount Thomas 60
12 New York Mountain 64
13 North Trail (Section 4: Son of Middle Creek
   to Red Sandstone) 68
14 Notch Mountain 72
15 Seven Sisters Lakes/Fall Creek Pass/
   Whitney Peak 76
16 Shrine Ridge and Holy Cross Overlook 80
17 Tuhare Lakes 84
18 Uneva Peak 88
19 Upper Piney River Trail 92
20 Vail Mountain—Eagle's Loop 96

About the Author 101
Checklist 103

ACKNOWLEDGMENTS

This book has certainly been a "labor of love." When I first agreed to take on the project, I thought, "How cool it would be to have my name on a book." Cut to 16 months later, after hundreds of e-mails and hundreds of hours of effort. Now it's no longer about the glory of publishing a book, but rather the wonderful memories brought about by documenting the trails that follow. Retracing past hikes, I reflect on what a special place I live in and how fortunate I am to have experienced most everything this book has to offer.

This project could not have been completed without the enthusiastic involvement of several Gore Range members who submitted trail descriptions, including helpful and accurate "beta" and colorful photos of the trails they hiked. While all of the contributors will be credited for their work, in various places in the book, I want to thank a few of them here: George Christman, not only for his trail submissions and photos, but especially for being the book's cartographer; photographers Michelle Cawood, Gene Marsh, Grace Wellwerts, and Scott McClarrinon—my friend, adventure buddy, and professional photographer. All of these folks provided vital photos that show readers why we selected particular trails for this book.

I also want to thank Series Editor John Gascoyne for his advice, assistance, and, most important, his patience and perseverance. Preparing this book wasn't easy, and I learned a lot during the process. Thanks also to Christian Green, publisher of Colorado Mountain Club Press, for his "hands-on" help, especially with many of the trail photos. Finally, thanks to the Colorado Mountain Club for their support of this project and, most important, their stewardship and continuing efforts to ensure this area is kept beautiful and accessible for those who wish to cherish it. Yes, this state is "Colorful Colorado" and Vail is a unique and valuable part.

Foreword

Surrounded by forest, high mountain peaks, deep cut valleys, high glacial-cut basins, and the secluded Holy Cross and Eagles Nest wilderness areas, visitors and residents of the Vail Valley are very fortunate to have an exciting array of hikes available to us. As with many popular areas, easily accessible trails can be loved to death. While much of the natural beauty remains on these overused trails, their diminished condition makes them less effective refuges from the hustle and bustle of urban life.

With this line of thought, we are omitting three of the four very popular trails along the East Vail Frontage Road: Booth Creek, Pitkin Lake, Bighorn Creek, and Deluge Lake/Gore Creek. While all four are certainly wonderful hikes, we have elected to include only the Booth Creek Trail. There are many other hidden hiking gems in this area, and we have sought to share some of them with you.

Many members of the Gore Range Group of the Colorado Mountain Club have called this valley home for years and truly appreciate its variety of hikes, from simple walks in the woods to remote adventures in the wild. In this book you will find a moderate hike/snowshoe experience in the Tenmile Range in our eastern-most reaches; a beautiful high-mountain stroll from Vail Pass; several mid-valley adventures into the wilderness areas; and, to the west—down valley—two of my favorites: a long summit "ridge hike" with 360° views, and a creek-side stroll where the destination is immaterial—it's all about the journey.

As you enjoy the exploration and adventure offered by this book, I'm sure you'll recognize the amazing splendor of Colorado's greater Vail Valley area.

NATHAN FREE
Gore Range Group,
The Colorado Mountain Club

Hikers Kim, Lisa, and their labs relax on the banks of Hunky Dory Lake.

THE BEST VAIL VALLEY HIKES

Introduction

(Please review this material carefully—it covers many topics that you should be familiar with before starting out on your first adventure.)

In this pack guide, we offer 20 of our area's best day hikes—with options for extensions and multi-day trips. Some of the hikes, intended for experienced trekkers, include undefined trails. Plan accordingly and be fully prepared.

The maps in this book can be augmented with the additional maps suggested at the beginning of each hike description. You can get up-to-date information from the U.S. Forest Service, just off I-70 in Minturn. This is especially helpful if you're planning an extended trip.

Most of our beautiful hikes take place on National Forest Service land and are within 30 minutes' drive time from Vail. Some of them, however, involve slow driving on unpaved surfaces and require up to an hour of travel time. Consult the "Getting There" section of your intended hike to approximate your required driving time.

For information on current conditions, call the U.S. Forest Service, 970-827-5715, or visit the White River National Forest hiking trails website. *(See below)*

TRAIL RATINGS

Wheelchair accessible—paved or graded and smooth surface with little or no elevation gain. These are also the easiest trails for younger hikers.

Easy—relatively smooth surface with few obstacles to step over; mild elevation gain, less than 200 feet per mile; good for family hiking.

Easy–moderate—a bit longer, slightly more demanding but still not too much for most hikers.

Moderate—the most common of mountain hiking trails—inconsistent conditions, including rocks, roots, ruts,

Parry's primrose, along the Shrine Ridge Trail.   PHOTO BY RITA THOMPSON

creek crossings and moderate elevation gain, up to 500 feet per mile. These offer the hiker a decent range of up-and-down real estate, passable water crossings, etc.

Moderate–difficult—these divide casual walkers from serious hikers. These trails can be distinguished by greater length, more serious elevation and, possibly, a bit of off-trail route finding where no obvious portion of a trail exists.

Difficult—by definition, these are challenging to most hikers. They can be longer, much higher, may contain some non-technical exposure, and possibly some challenging route finding. Trails may be very inconsistent or non-existent in places. Unless otherwise described, these are still intended to be single-day experiences.

THE TRAILS IN THIS PACK GUIDE, BY DEGREE OF DIFFICULTY

Wheelchair—Gore Valley Trail, Grizzly Creek (0.25 mile option), Holy Cross Overlook, Vail Mountain—Eagle's Loop

Easy—Mayflower Gulch, North Trail, Shrine Ridge

Easy–moderate—Corral Creek, Lionshead Rock, Upper Piney River, Vail Mountain options

Moderate—Booth River Creek Trail, Bowman's Shortcut to Top of the World, Grizzly Creek, Lonesome Lake, Mount Thomas, New York Mountain, Uneva Peak

Moderate–difficult—Booth Creek, Lake Charles/Mystic Island Lake, Missouri Pass/Fancy Pass, Notch Mountain, Seven Sisters Lakes/Fall Creek Pass/Whitney Peak, Tuhare Lakes

SEASONS

Summer/fall—The upper elevations melt off later in the season and gain snow earlier, providing the best escape from the heat of summer. All of our trails are accessible during this time of year.

Winter/early spring—While some trails are not easily accessible during this season, many are less crowded and offer a unique and varied experience. I recommend adding 20 to 50 percent to your estimated travel time, depending on whether the snow surface is packed down or not. Some suggestions for this experience: Booth Creek, Corral Creek, Gore Valley Trail, Grizzly Creek, Lionshead Rock, Lonesome Lake (see options nearby), Mayflower Gulch, Missouri Pass, North Trail, and Vail Mountain—Eagle's Loop.

HIKING SPEED—RULE OF THUMB

Allow 1 hour for each 1,000 feet of elevation gain and another hour for every two miles of distance. While most local hikers will exceed this pace, I find it a practical guideline for the average, fit visitor.

The Ten Essentials Systems

This pack guide is published by the Colorado Mountain Club—now in its 100th year of fostering safe practices and environmental stewardship in the wild areas of our state. Every hiker—experienced or beginner—will benefit by studying these principles, practicing them, and teaching them to others.

Read carefully—these are the things you really want to carry:

1. **Hydration.** Each day hiker should carry a minimum of two quarts, or liters, of water. In more arid regions, carry more. A good practice is to have lots of extra water in your vehicle—drink a good deal of it before setting out, and save some for the end of your experience. Consider purchasing a CamelBak® or similar soft carrier that fits inside of, or attached to, your daypack—having a drinking tube close to your face while you are hiking is a great way to stay hydrated. Whatever you do, continue drinking while you are on the trail—if you wait until you are thirsty, you've waited too long.

2. **Nutrition.** Don't skimp on ingesting energy-producing foods. Eat a large and healthy breakfast before hiking. Pack a good lunch with lots of fruits, vegetables, and carbohydrates. Carry quick energy snacks such as trail mix and nutrition bars—as much as anything this can help keep your mind clear for decision making.

3. **Sun protection.** Apply—and re-apply—sunscreen with at least a 45 SPF rating. Apply lip balm. Wear sunglasses and a wide-brimmed hat. Keep in mind that the sun's UV rays at 10,000 feet are roughly 25 percent stronger than at sea level, and if you are around snow, as much as 90 percent of the sunlight is reflected back a second time.

4. **Insulation.** Carry extra clothing to fit different critical needs. Colorado's weather can change in very short intervals; be prepared to cope with nature's surprises. More than anything else, you want to stay warm and dry, so pack accordingly. Cotton is the serious enemy here, leave it home; wool and synthetic materials will serve you well. Layering is critical, especially in cold or wet weather; put clothing on or take it off as the situation changes. Hypothermia—a potentially life-threatening decrease in body temperature—is most active at the top of your head. Carry a warm hat, warm gloves, and an extra pair of socks. Be prepared for wet weather with a parka or shell and rain pants. Experienced hikers will spend the little extra time needed to make clothing changes as often as their situation requires.

5. **Navigation.** Basic route-finding abilities are a critical skill for all hikers, even on what seem to be clearly marked trails. Learn minimal proficiency with a map and compass. Before you hike, use a map of the entire area and study your route. A global positioning system (GPS) device can add to your capabilities.

6. **Illumination.** A flashlight, with extra batteries, is an essential part of your gear. A better idea is to carry a headlamp, which allows both hands to be free. Nighttime hiking can be hazardous; avoid it except in emergencies.

7. **First Aid.** There are good hiker's first aid kits available or you can create one that best fits your needs and preferences. Consider including:
   - A plastic container of alcohol and/or hydrogen peroxide—useful for cleaning a wound, dealing with insect bites, etc.
   - A bandana—has many uses, including as an arm sling or emergency tourniquet

- Duct tape—can go over a blister or wound, provide emergency repairs, and serve many other uses
- Hygiene supplies—liquid soap, latex gloves, toilet paper, and Ziploc bags—nothing is left in the woods
- A chart or booklet on how to deal with medical emergencies

8. **Fire.** Open fires in the woods should be considered dangerous and avoided when at all possible. If emergency circumstances force you to build an open fire—for warmth or cooking—use all possible care. Carry fire ribbon or waterproof matches in a watertight container. Hardened tree sap and dry pine needles can help get a fire going. If you will be cooking on the trail, use a hiker's portable stove and fuel in a very tight metal container.

9. **Repair kit and emergency tools.** Carry a small pocket knife or, better, a multi-use tool with a decent blade. Duct tape and electrical tape can serve many purposes. Carry a signal mirror and whistle in your tool kit.

10. **Emergency shelter.** Carry some nylon cord and a space blanket or a bivouac sack. A large plastic leaf bag can have multiple uses—temporary rain shelter, a cover for your pack, or a survival shelter. Use the bag on your way out to carry trash left behind by less thoughtful hikers.

OTHER USEFUL SAFETY MEASURES

Tell someone where you'll be hiking and when you plan to return.

Leave a note on your dashboard, readable from outside your vehicle, that provides information about your hike—where you are heading, when you will return, how many are in your party, and contact information for family or friends.

Bleached cottonwood makes a nice contrast against another Colorado "Bluebird Day" and the towering cliffs that form the narrow valley of Grizzly Creek. PHOTO BY NATHAN FREE

Carry a SPOT—this satellite-activated personal locator can tell emergency personnel that you need help and where to find you. These devices retail for around $100 or more, but can save lives. When you're not hiking, keep the device in your vehicle for emergency use.

A NOTE ON HYPOTHERMIA

This is the phenomenon where wetness or cold, or a combination of the two, chills the body and results in a lowering of its core temperature. When not addressed, hypothermia can be fatal. Water is the severest conductor of heat loss and more cases of hypothermia have been recorded in the summer than in the winter. Cotton is considered a killer—it retains water and chills the body. Wool and synthetics tend to wick the water away and can retain heat even when damp. Gear up at the first sign of rain; change out of wet clothes at the first opportunity.

LEAVE NO TRACE

Trashing wild places is not an option: if you pack it in, pack it out—leave only footprints:

- Plan ahead and prepare for the cleanest possible adventure.
- Stay on the trail and don't shortcut on switchbacks; camp on durable surfaces, such as rock or sand. Above timberline, hike on rocks and avoid damaging the tundra. When more than one person is off trail, spread out so you don't start destructive new "social" trails.
- Dispose of all waste properly, including that deposited by your dog. Pack it in, pack it out.
- Leave what you find—look at it, take a photo, and leave it for the next person.
- Minimize campfire impacts—think small, keep the fuel within the fire circle, and unless it is a permanent fire pit, destroy all traces of your fire before leaving your campsite. Forest fires have started from small camp fires; be extremely cautious in this regard.
- Respect wildlife—don't feed them anything and don't intrude on their feeding and breeding areas. Moose deserve your complete respect; they are considered the most dangerous creatures in the Colorado woods.
- Be considerate of animals and other humans in the woods—no radios or other unnecessary noise. Part of the lure of the woods is the healing sound of wind through the trees, the murmur of a stream, or no noise at all.

Camping and Backpacking Information

WILDERNESS AREAS—EAGLES NEST AND HOLY CROSS IN THE VAIL VALLEY AREA

There are no designated campsites—which you will find in a wilderness travel zone—but there are many obvious sites with fire rings where other folks have camped before. Adhering to the "Leave No Trace" philosophy will have you camping in these sites.

Campsites in designated wilderness areas must be 200 feet or more from any water source—i.e., stream or lake—and 200 feet or more from any established trail. In all instances, campfires must be at least 0.25 miles (440 yards) from any treeline. Check before you leave to determine current rules and restrictions. Wilderness group size is limited to 12 "beating hearts." This includes livestock—dogs, horses, llamas, etc.—as well as humans.

While dogs are permitted here, they must be kept on a leash that is no longer than 6 feet.

Bikes are not permitted in any designated wilderness area.

BACKCOUNTRY CAMPING

Dispersed—i.e., not clustered—backcountry camping is allowed in the Eagles Nest Wilderness Area. See above for wilderness camping rules. When you are planning your trip, contact the Holy Cross Ranger District (970-827-5715) for the latest information on weather, trail conditions, and trail-specific guidelines. Their office is open from 8 a.m. to 4 p.m. on weekdays.

For those not wishing to camp in the backcountry, there are several developed campgrounds within the White River National Forest. Contact the Holy Cross Ranger District for information on these sites.

Wildflowers and an unnamed summit along the Lonesome Lake Trail.
PHOTO BY CAROL GLASSON

GORE CREEK CAMPGROUND—FACILITIES AND CAMPGROUND INFORMATION

The Gore Creek Campground is located on Bighorn Road, 2.5 miles east of Exit 180 off of I-70. It's located just past the Gore Creek trailhead and has 25 campsites with picnic tables and fire grates. There is a vault toilet.

FISHING INFORMATION

With a valid Colorado license, fishing is permitted along almost all creeks and lakes. Single-day licenses can be purchased at the Sports Authority in Avon.

CONTACT INFORMATION

Holy Cross Ranger District
24747 US Hwy 24
Minturn, CO 81645
970-827-5715

White River National Forest
900 Grand Ave.
P.O. Box 948
Glenwood Springs, CO 81602
970-945-2521

Caveat on maps and map scales: In this pack guide, we have endeavored in all instances to provide the most accurate information possible. This striving for accuracy includes the map segments that follow each trail description. Many of the trails indicated by the red lines, however, include contours, ups and downs, and switchbacks that cannot be depicted on a small map. Thus, with some maps, you may find what appears to be a variance between the stated length of the trail and its length when compared to the scale indicator.

For every trail described in this guide, we list relevant maps of the area you will be hiking in, such as Trails Illustrated and USGS maps. It is always a good practice to secure these larger maps, study them, and understand where the smaller map fits within the larger map. The best practice is to carry both maps on your hike.

1. Booth Creek Trail

BY NATHAN FREE

MAPS	Trails Illustrated, Vail/Frisco/Dillon, Number 108 USGS, Vail Pass/Red Cliff Trails, 7.5 minute Latitude 40, Vail & Eagle Trails
ELEVATION GAIN	1,600 feet—Falls 3,080 feet—Lake
RATING	Moderate—Falls Moderate–difficult—Lake
ROUND-TRIP DISTANCE	4.0 miles—Falls 8.6 miles—Lake
ROUND-TRIP TIME	3 hours—Falls 7 hours—Lake
NEAREST LANDMARK	Town of Vail

COMMENT: The trail along Booth Creek is one of the most popular hiking trails in the Vail area, because the ascent up the beautiful valley, with Vail Mountain at your back, is really quite special. Having accessible water is an added bonus. Most hikers are happy just to make it to the lovely 60-foot Booth Falls and enjoy lunch on one of the rocks overhanging the water. If you venture on toward the lake, you will have the trail mostly to yourself. Booth Lake is nestled into a large cirque in the upper reaches of the deep, narrow valley containing Booth Creek. Almost the entire trail is in the Eagles Nest Wilderness Area.

This is a wonderful hike almost any time of year. Wildflowers—which thrive on all the moisture from the creeks—are usually crazy pretty. The abundance of aspen trees in the valley creates a blaze of color in the fall. In winter the trail is usually packed down and snowshoeing conditions are ideal, mostly protected from the winds and full of south-facing

Booth Lake, looking up to the ridge crossing to Upper Piney.

PHOTO BY SCOTT MCCLARRINON

sun. I have even enjoyed nighttime "shoes" here. Do be aware of crossing below slide paths as you venture up. When I'm traveling in the snow, I usually add 20 percent over the time I estimate for hiking on dry land.

GETTING THERE: The trailhead is only about 2 miles east of Vail Village, on the South Frontage Road, about 0.5 mile past the Vail Golf Course. After crossing underneath the interstate, to the north side, take the second left onto Booth Falls Road. Drive up about 1 block and you'll find the marked trailhead, with limited parking. Note, this is also 1.0 mile west of Exit 180 on I-70 (along the North Frontage Road). If the two small lots are full, overflow parking can be found at the nearby Vail Mountain School.

THE ROUTE: From the trailhead, at 8,400 feet, be prepared to start gaining elevation immediately, as the trail begins with several switchbacks between the parking lot and the wilderness entrance sign 0.25 mile up the trail. The traffic noise from the interstate competes with the sound of Booth Creek for only about the first 0.5 mile, and then you are engulfed in nature: the creek, rustling trees, birds, and radiant wildflowers.

The grade is moderate and steady over the first 1.5 miles as you travel through aspens and open fields of the widening valley, framed by towering, red-hued walls. The grade then steepens and grows rugged over the next 0.5 mile, as the pine forest thickens and the trail approaches the falls, at 9,720 feet. Definitely take a moment to enjoy the views below and above the falls.

If your destination is the lake, be ready for a more rugged trail, as it is steeper and less maintained above the falls. At 2.5 miles, there's a break in the timber as you move from one shelf/basin to the next. At 3.0 miles the grade is moderate and the views are more open. Then, at 4.0 miles, the trail becomes steep and twisting as you approach the grassy eastern shores of the lake, at 11,480 feet, right about tree line. The area around the lake is open and easy to explore, as are the open, flowery slopes above. There is a low ridge above the lake's south shore that provides a wonderful vantage of the entire basin as well as a view back down the valley toward the Vail ski area and Mount of the Holy Cross beyond.

Once they have taken time to explore, most folks return along the route they took to get there.

Note: A very adventure-filled loop continues up to the ridge above the lake. This loop travels through the lower point/saddle, down to Upper Piney Lake, and then on down to Piney Lake itself. Hikers planning this journey should leave a shuttle vehicle there; for most, this is a multi-day trip into the remote wilderness. For me, it was one of my most memorable Vail area adventures.

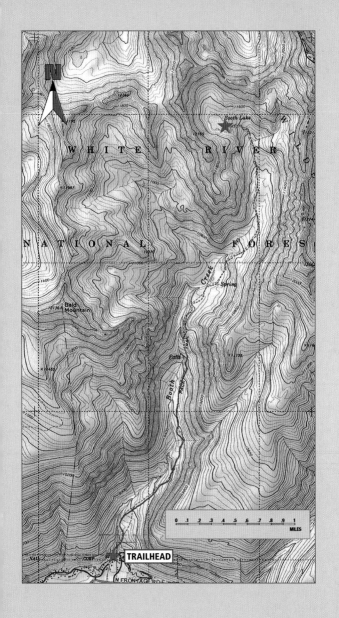

TRAILHEAD

2. Bowman's Shortcut to Top of the World

BY RITA THOMPSON

MAPS	Trails Illustrated, Vail/Frisco/ Dillon, Number 108 USGS Vail Pass/Red Cliff, 7.5 minute Latitude 40, Vail & Eagle Trails
ELEVATION GAIN	In 1,200 feet; out 350 feet
RATING	Moderate
ROUND-TRIP DISTANCE	7.5 miles
ROUND-TRIP TIME	6–7 hours
NEAREST LANDMARK	Vail Pass

COMMENT: Enjoy spectacular views of the famous Back Bowls of Vail Ski Area and the Gore Range. Huge fields of wildflowers bloom profusely in the open meadows from mid-June through September. You will see a few bikes on this trail, because biking is allowed. Winter snowshoe and cross-country ski access is available only from Vail Rest Area as a departure point.

GETTING THERE: From the Town of Vail, drive east on I-70. At 14.5 miles, take Exit 190, Vail Pass Rest Area (15 minutes). At the stop sign, turn right (restrooms on the loop to the left). Take the fork to the right onto the Shrine Pass, Red Cliff FDR#709, dirt road and continue for 3.9 miles (15–20 minutes), staying left (on the main road) at the next fork, and continuing past the Shrine Ridge Trailhead parking lot. Just past Mount of the Holy Cross Overlook Trailhead, turn right at the sign that says Bowman's Shortcut Trailhead. In 0.6 mile, there is a lesser fork to the right; do not take it.

Zoom of Vail's Back Bowls and Gore Range.

PHOTO BY RITA THOMPSON

Rather, continue on for 0.1 mile to the marked Bowman's Shortcut Trailhead sign on the right. This is 4.6 miles total from I-70 (25–35 minutes).

THE ROUTE: Bowman's Shortcut Trailhead sign (elevation 10,860 feet) states 4.5 miles to Elk Pass (and the trail crossing there, carrying the same name). Since the views are better from the ridge, our hike will be only 3.75 miles one way; shorter by simply turning around at any point. At the beginning, the trail is slightly steep and rocky for a short distance. It then becomes very pleasant with pine needles to soften your step through a beautiful lodgepole pine forest. Highway I-70 is visible far below on the right side (northeast). With varying grades of uphill steepness, the next part of the hike is a series of about a dozen switchbacks. The trees get thicker and taller as the trail ascends.

Eventually, the trail makes its way to a summit ridge of sorts, and the Copper Mountain Ski Area will come into view on your left (south), along with the Tenmile Range. On the right, the Gore Range is spectacular, especially where the trail is above a steep slope, and you can see over the tree tops. Eventually the trail levels out at the "Top of the World" (elevation 11,611 feet). Although not as climactic as the name implies, you are essentially at "the top".

As you continue along the ridge, Mount of the Holy Cross is on the left, and the trail undulates 100' down and 250' up for 0.75 mile to the highest ridge, elevation 11,710 feet. At this point look left between two trees toward a ridge where the towers of the Skyline Express chairlift in the Blue Sky Basin portion of Vail Ski Area are visible. Walk to the right off the trail, out into a high meadow, for a great view of Benchmark, a/k/a Red Mountain, and the Back Bowls of Vail. From here you can also see the rock formation that forms the "China Wall" of China Bowl, which continues above the Poma ski lift that accesses the Mongolia Bowls.

When you return to the trail the view of the Back Bowls gets better the farther you go. In the next mile, the trail undulates 250 feet down and 200 feet up until you are at 11,618 feet. Any elevation you lose will have to be climbed on the way out. (If you were to go all the way to Two Elk Pass, elevation 11,000 feet, you would have to ascend at least 950 feet going out.)

To hike out, reverse your route and follow the same well-marked trail along the ridge. Go down through the switch-backs and slightly up as you approach the trailhead where your car is parked.

Note: From May 6 to July 1, during elk calving season, the Back Bowls of Vail are closed, but Bowman's Shortcut and Two Elk Trail east to Vail Recreation Trail remain open.

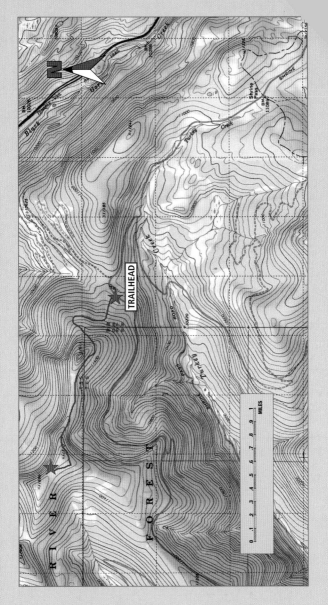

TRAILHEAD

rral Creek

BY JIM CUNNINGHAM

MAPS	Trails Illustrated, Vail/Frisco/ Dillon, Number 108 Latitude 40, Vail & Eagle Trails
ELEVATION GAIN	510 feet
RATING	Easy–moderate
ROUND-TRIP DISTANCE	4 miles
ROUND-TRIP TIME	2 hours
NEAREST LANDMARK	Vail Pass

COMMENT: Located just over a ridge to the northeast from Vail Pass, Corral Creek is surprisingly isolated from I-70 noise. This hike is one of the easier high elevation hikes in the area and affords spectacular views. It is also a very nice snowshoe or backcountry ski trail.

The Corral Creek hike is also the standard route to summit Uneva Peak (12,522 feet). The main trail goes up a ridge leading into a bowl below Uneva Peak. This bowl, while generally safe for winter travel, can be dangerous during high avalanche conditions and should be avoided then. The hike can be accessed from a few different points but the most popular one, described here, starts from the Vail Pass Rest Area. For summer hiking the area is free, but during winter a "use fee" is required, currently $6 per day or $40 for a season pass. Although the area south of the interstate is popular with snowmobile users, motorized vehicles are prohibited in the area north (where this trail leads). The trail is an easy summer hike and a moderate cross-country ski or snowshoe trip.

GETTING THERE: The trailhead is easy to find, whether you're coming from the east or west. Go to the Vail Pass Rest Area,

The old corrals, for which the area is named.   PHOTO BY SELMA KRISTEL

on the southwest side of I-70, at Exit 190. There are two parking lots in the rest area, upper and lower. The usual place to park is the upper lot, but that can fill up, especially in winter, and you may have to park in the lower lot, by the restrooms. The trailhead is across the interstate, to the north at the end of the overpass.

THE ROUTE: The trailhead is apparent in the summer, but may be behind a wall of snow in winter. There is a pole with a blue diamond near the start of the trail and other blue markers along the way. The trail begins by heading steeply uphill, but soon levels off at a junction of two trails: one heading downhill and one going more uphill. It doesn't matter which you take, because both end up in essentially the same place. If there has been much rain, or if the snow is still melting, you will encounter a willow bog that is relatively easy to skirt.

Keep following the trail until you break out of the trees into a wide-open view of the mountains. Here the trail joins an old road. Turn left on this old road and follow it for about 0.3 mile, where the trail then goes slightly downhill and takes a sharp right turn. In summer the trail is obvious; in winter it's obvious only if the trail has been used and packed down.

THE BEST VAIL VALLEY HIKES   29

Looking through one of the many
burnt remains of the area.

PHOTO BY JIM CUNNINGHAM

After the trail turns right, down the hill, it goes slightly uphill and then turns back to the left and continues uphill.

The trail continues on a slight uphill for about 0.25 mile, at which point you will see a steep hill in front of you. The trail takes a sharp right at this point and goes around the side of this hill. Follow the trail a short distance and you'll see the clear remnants of the old road again, going to the left uphill. This is the trail. From here on you will be following a ridge going uphill. There is a slight downhill section where you cross a small creek, but the general trend is uphill on the ridge.

Resist the temptation to take any trails heading to the right from this trail, because you want to go directly uphill following the ridge. The trail will head up this ridge until you top out in an open area. If you start going downhill, you've gone too far. The top of the ridge is the end of the Corral Creek hike.

At this point you have tremendous views of the Vail Valley, the backside of Vail Ski Resort, and much of the Gore Range. Look back and you'll see Copper Mountain and Jacque Peak. This is a great lunch spot.

Return to the trailhead the same way you came up. One potentially tricky spot is where the first part of the trail connects with the old road. Most of the time the sharp right turn off the old road is clear, but it is, of course, possible to miss. If you do keep going on the old road, you will eventually pass the old corrals (the area's namesake) and connect with I-70 about a mile down from where you parked; then you can cross under the interstate, intersect with the paved Recreation Path, and return to Vail Pass (heading northwest).

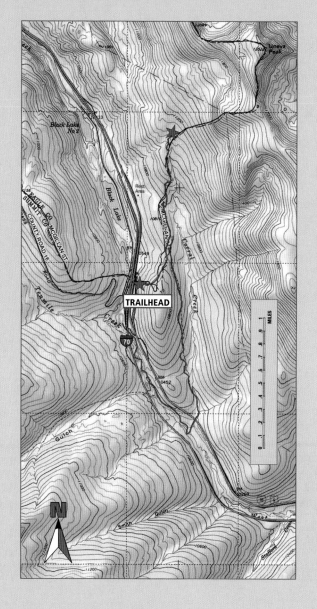

TRAILHEAD

MILES

N

4. Gore Valley Trail

BY COLLEEN WIDLAK

MAPS	Trails Illustrated, Vail/Frisco/Dillon, Number 108 Latitude 40, Vail & Eagle Trails Colorado Trails, Recreation Topo Map Vail Town Map: http://www.coloradoinfo.com/vail/town-map
ELEVATION GAIN	Minimal
RATING	Easy, wheelchair accessible
ROUND-TRIP DISTANCE	4.4 miles
ROUND-TRIP TIME	1.5–2.5 hours
NEAREST LANDMARK	Town of Vail, municipal golf course

COMMENT: The Gore Valley Trail is a paved recreation path stretching from West Vail to the summit of Vail Pass. This short section is our favorite because, without having to leave the Town of Vail you can enjoy beaver ponds, a crystal-clear stream, aspen groves, views of Grand Traverse Peak, and fine homes, all along the Gore Creek.

The trail winds through the Vail Golf Course and is wheelchair accessible. Pedestrians and bicyclists share this rolling, paved path, so be sure to stay to your right or you will frequently hear "on your left" as the cyclists wheel past you.

GETTING THERE: From the roundabout in Vail Village, travel east on Frontage Road, approximately 1.5 miles, to Vail Valley Drive. Turn right on Vail Valley Drive and continue past the Vail Golf Course and clubhouse to the cul-de-sac. Park here and proceed to the well-marked trailhead. Many visitors choose to park at the golf course and walk 0.25 mile down the

Gore Range.

PHOTO BY MICHELLE CAWOOD

quiet neighborhood street, enjoying the attractive gardens and the large aspen grove on their way to the trailhead.

THE ROUTE: Begin at mile 7.5 of the Gore Valley Trail. The total distance for this section of the trail/bike path is 2.2 miles. You'll encounter a gradual incline and rolling terrain at the beginning, but the trail will become level after the first 0.5 mile.

Your experience will be greatly affected by the season. In spring and early summer, as the snow pack in the higher terrain rapidly melts, the sounds of the I-70 freeway traffic are relatively muted by the rushing water of Gore Creek. Also, early in the season the waterfalls are more grandiose as they cascade over nearby cliffs.

Later in the season, the variety of wildflowers creates an eye-catching and restful landscape. The stunning gold of the aspen trees along parts of the trail will delight you through early fall. The trail remains open in winter for cross-country skiing and snowshoeing.

The trail provides spectacular views of the Gore Range. Wildlife often can be spotted, including inhabitants of the beaver ponds. Listen for woodpeckers and chickadees to add to your nature experience.

Gore Creek as seen from the trail's Eastern Portal.

PHOTO BY MICHELLE CAWOOD

As you make your way up and down this 2.2-mile section of the Gore Creek Trail, you will travel through aspen groves and meadows. Picnic tables, park benches, and picturesque bridges invite you to relax and enjoy the wonderful views. A log house with a sod roof provides an interesting example of mountain architecture. Continue until mile marker 9, where you will arrive at Memorial Park. Stroll through this 11-acre retreat where Vail citizens are remembered with their names and philosophies inscribed in stone. This area also includes a memorial park for pets.

The last 0.25 mile of the trail closely follows the creek. The rock beaches and formations along the bank offer other pleasing rest stops before you reach the end of this hike at Big Horn Road in East Vail (Exit 180 off of I-70). If you left a second car here, your hike is finished; otherwise, enjoy the scenery in reverse as you head back to your car in the cul-de-sac.

AN OPTIONAL ROUTE: If you prefer, you can start this trail at Exit 180 off I-70 at Big Horn Road, just off the exit. Cross Big Horn Road and hike the trail in the reverse of the above route. By starting at mile marker 9.5, the east end of the trail, you will avoid the slight uphill climb found at mile marker 8.0. Head west and enjoy all of the sights in the reverse order.

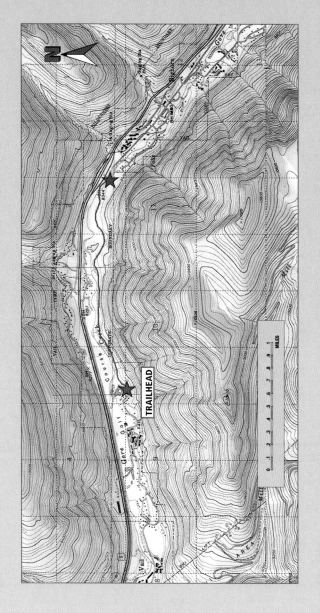

TRAILHEAD

MILES

0 .1 .2 .3 .4 .5 .6 .7 .8 .9 1

5. Grizzly Creek

BY JUDITH RAU

MAPS	Trails Illustrated, Flat Tops SE/ Glenwood Canyon, Number 123
ELEVATION GAIN	1,800 feet
RATING	Easy–moderate
ROUND-TRIP DISTANCE	7 miles from rest area
ROUND-TRIP TIME	3–4 hours
NEAREST LANDMARK	12 miles west of Dotsero, 5 miles east of Glenwood Springs

COMMENT: The Grizzly Creek Trailhead is in the midst of the splendor of Glenwood Canyon. This canyon, cut by the Colorado River, provides the surroundings for a beautiful drive, and can be considered a destination in itself. Starting at 5,900 feet, the first mile of Grizzly Creek provides a hiking trail that is easy traveling and very scenic. This section is popular with families and dog owners, because there are picnic tables located right next to the creek and dogs are allowed off leash. Fishing is also enjoyed along the creek banks. Unless you plan to travel beyond the described route, there is little need to consult your map because the trail is obvious and follows the creek, which is never out of sight or earshot.

During the Pleistocene Era, Grizzly Creek carved this narrow valley as it cascaded down from the snow-covered Flat Tops to the north to meet with the Colorado River. Today, you'll see a nature photographer's paradise that includes huge boulders, fallen cottonwoods, and a variety of wildflowers and flowering shrubs.

Spring gets a head start along the creek, due to the lower elevation along the Colorado River, and you are able to

Grizzly Creek, in late summer. PHOTO BY NATHAN FREE

hike much sooner than is possible in the Vail area. In peak summer, try to be on the trail by sunrise—you'll miss the crowds and you just might see some Rocky Mountain bighorn sheep.

More recent history of Glenwood Canyon: It's not clear when the trail evolved from a footpath or wagon path through the canyon. In 1906, however, the construction of the hydroelectric Shoshone Power Plant to deliver power to Glenwood Springs resulted in rapid development and a maintained dirt road. During the Depression, $1.5 million was apportioned for the first widening and paving of the canyon road. The improvements were celebrated on August 1, 1938, and, from that time until the 1960s, US 6-24 through the canyon saw few changes. Eventually, officials decided to extend the interstate system, and construction of the present multi-level, divided highway began in 1980 and was completed in 1992—at a cost of $490 million. (Some historical data compiled from the writings of M. A. Salek.)

GETTING THERE: From Vail, take I-70 west for 55 miles to Grizzly Creek Rest Area, Exit 121. As you enter the rest area, go past the first parking lot on your left, then turn right and go under the highway to the hiking trail parking.

THE ROUTE: After the first mile, described above, the trail becomes more rugged and more strenuous. As the canyon narrows and the creek becomes wilder, large boulders create scenic waterfalls and clear pools. The trail climbs upward and skirts the steep-sided slopes, which are topped by sheer limestone cliffs.

The valley is covered by a variety of flora, from conifers and large cottonwoods along the creek bed to shrubs such as serviceberries, chokecherries, mountain maple, mountain mahogany, and scrub oak.

After about 3.5 miles of alternating steep climbs and level stretches, the trail ends between two "house-sized" boulders right at the creek. The large black pipe across the creek is used to pipe water from Grizzly Creek through the mountain to No Name Creek, which provides water to Glenwood Springs. Below this pipe are some old boards left over from the original scaffolding used for the water sluice. This is as far as most hikers go.

This trail can be enjoyed year around—from spring, when the runoff swells the creek, to autumn, when blazing colors light up the trees. Snowshoes or boot cleats may be useful in winter. During a snowy winter, be aware that snow slides can occur along some of the exposed trail sections.

Return to the trailhead by simply retracing your steps.

An Extended Route: Hardier, more experienced adventurers can extend the described hike another 2.5 miles beyond the water pipe to a group of waterfalls at 8,600 feet. This results in a total gain of 2,500 vertical feet. Ultimately, the narrow and steep-walled canyon climbs and expands into the Flat Tops at 10,000 to 10,500 feet. A multiple-day through-hike to Coffee Pot Road is a possibility; otherwise just turn around and enjoy the downhill trek back to the canyon floor.

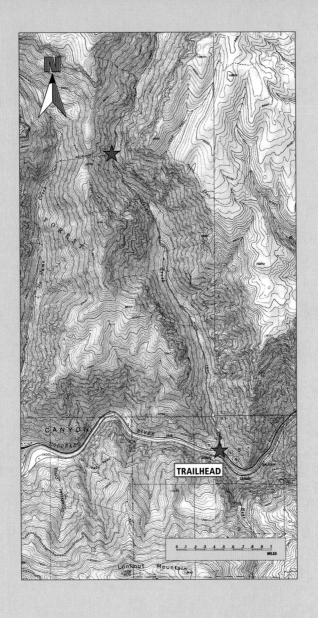

TRAILHEAD

6. Lake Charles/ Mystic Island Lake

BY CINDY LAGACE

MAPS	Trails Illustrated, Holy Cross/ Ruedi Reservoir, Number 126 USGS, Crooked Creek Pass and Mt. Jackson, 7.5 minute Latitude 40, Vail & Eagle Trails
ELEVATION GAIN	2,055 feet—Lakes Charles 2,280 feet—Mystic Island Lake
RATING	Moderate
ROUND-TRIP DISTANCE	9.2 miles
ROUND-TRIP TIME	7–9 hours
NEAREST LANDMARK	Town of Eagle

COMMENT: This hike is a must for fishermen and photographers. The trail accesses good fishing in East Brush Creek, which has rainbow, brook, and brown trout. Lake Charles and Mystic Island Lake both have Colorado cutthroat trout. Lake Charles has a spectacular view of Fools Peak (12,947 feet) and a glacial cirque at the end of the valley. Mystic Island Lake has a glacial tarn to the southwest and, at 13,043 feet, Eagle Peak rises behind the lake. There are several campsites at the lake, especially on the north side of the trail.

The beauty of this trail begins at the trailhead parking lot, which overlooks a serene beaver pond. The trail follows East Brush Creek all the way up to both Lake Charles (4.6 miles/ elevation 11,055 feet) and Mystic Island Lake (5.6 miles/ elevation 11,280 feet) in the Holy Cross Wilderness Area.

This trail is open to hiking only, so it is very pleasant and peaceful here. Although it is heavily used in the summer, most of the trail's traffic seems to be day hikers, especially

Fools Peak catching the early morning light.

fishermen. The trail is in good condition and easy to follow so there are no route-finding issues.

GETTING THERE: From Vail, travel west on I-70 and take Eagle Exit 147. Turn left over the highway, on Eby Creek Road, traveling to Hwy 6. Go west at the roundabout and take the first left onto Capitol Street. Continue through town for 0.8 mile and, at a three-way stop, turn left onto Brush Creek Road. From here, follow signs to Sylvan Lake State Park. Continue past the visitors' center; at mile 15.3, there will be a "Y." Take the left fork onto East Brush Creek Road, FDR 415, and drive 6 miles until you reach the parking lot at Fulford Cave Campground. The parking will be on the right, along with the trailhead information board. This is a spacious and well-used parking lot, because it serves the Lake Charles Trailhead, the Ironedge Trailhead, and the Fulford Cave.

THE ROUTE: Start your hike from the trailhead/parking lot at 9,000 feet. The trailhead is close to the gate, just to the right of the information board. Be sure to take the left trail,

Beaver pond along the route.

PHOTO BY CINDY LAGACE

because the trail to the right is the Ironedge—FDT 1873. The trail begins in a shady aspen grove, and changes to dense pine, spruce, and fir. Along the way, the wildflowers are splendid, and you will enjoy the sounds of East Brush Creek almost the entire hike. Within the first mile/hour of hiking, you will encounter a "washed out" bridge. There is an arrow posted on a tree leading you to the current trail on the left side of the river. Do NOT cross the river. Also, at about one hour into the hike you will enter the Holy Cross Wilderness Area.

The trail continues a gradual climb, with grades less than 10 percent, and there are only two sustained, steep, uphill climbs, as well as a few rocky areas with exposed tree roots and the like. Along the way, you will cross a few tributary streams and find many picturesque pools and waterfalls, but you should not have to ever actually cross Brush Creek. Return the way you came.

For added adventure: Along the trail to Lake Charles is the turning-off point to summit Gold Dust Peak, at an elevation of 13,365 feet. This side provides a somewhat more hospitable approach to this beautiful peak than found from other directions. As mentioned, Mystic Island Lake, just another mile up the trail, is a worthwhile extension.

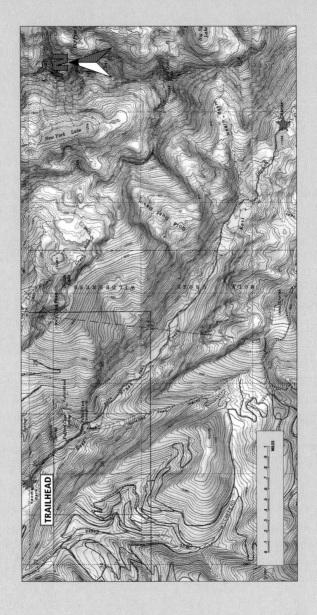

7. Lionshead Rock

BY GEORGE CHRISTMAN

MAPS	Trails Illustrated, Vail/Frisco/Dillon, Number 108 Latitude 40, Vail & Eagle Trails Recreation Topo Map
ELEVATION GAIN	1,580 feet
RATING	Moderate
ROUND-TRIP DISTANCE	3.88 miles
ROUND-TRIP TIME	2.5–3 hours
NEAREST LANDMARK	Town of Minturn

COMMENT: The views on this hike are excellent. Notch Mountain, the Mount of the Holy Cross, and Mount Jackson in the Holy Cross Wilderness Area can be seen to the south. Meadow Mountain and the Beaver Creek Ski Area are to the west. Castle Peak, near the Flat Tops Wilderness, can be seen to the northwest. Mount Powell and Vail's Eagle's Nest Gondola area can be seen to the north and east.

The hike up is a good workout. The trail is protected from harsh weather by the trees and sides of the mountain. There are a variety of trees and flowering plants along the way. In the late summer, thimbleberries are abundant along the first several miles of the trek. In winter, elk and other animals can be found foraging for food along the hillsides. Due to the lower elevation and the hike's western exposure, snow clears from this trail relatively early for our area.

GETTING THERE: You're heading high above Minturn. Take Exit 171 off I-70 and drive south on US 24 to Minturn. When you first enter the town, turn sharply left, on South Main Street, and go across the Eagle River. Just past the Minturn Saloon, turn right on Railroad Avenue. Go across the three sets of

At top, looking down to meadows of the old lettuce farms, and the town of Minturn.   PHOTO BY GEORGE CHRISTMAN

railroad tracks to Taylor Street. Follow Taylor Street in a northerly direction, to the trailhead at the end of the road. (From I-70, the trailhead is 2.2 miles.)

THE ROUTE: You will be hiking 1.94 miles and achieving a gain of 1,500 feet, thus the average pitch/slope of the hike is steady and steep. The trailhead elevation is 7,852 feet, and the top of Lionshead Rock is 9,352 feet. Hiking up to Lionshead Rock entails between one and one and a half hours of steady exertion.

Note: This trek is accessed in both summer and winter. The grade in some sections is over 30 percent, so skiing up or biking up to Lionshead Rock is not typically done. However, skiing and riding down this trail, from above, occurs year round; so be aware and look uphill.

If you plan to snowshoe up this trail in winter, note that it is popular for others to ski or ride out of Game Creek Bowl, down into the town of Minturn. The skiers' run-out will share only the lower section of the Lionshead Rock Trail,

Along the trail, with Mount of the Holy Cross on the horizon.
PHOTO BY GEORGE CHRISTMAN

as it follows along Game Creek. This is normally an end-of-day event, with the reward being a visit to the Minturn Saloon.

There is limited parking at the trailhead. Respect the private property areas and follow the signs for the Game Creek Trail. There are plenty of signs and blue diamonds on the trees to mark the correct path as it skirts the private property areas.

This route follows the Game Creek Trail for about the first 20 minutes until you come to a Y in the trail. Leave the Game Creek Trail and take the unsigned Lionshead/Cougar Ridge Trail right across the creek. You will see an old piece of rusting riveted water pipe next to the crossing. Head up through the thimbleberry and aspen area. On the aspen bark, you will see signs of elk grazing—this part of the hill is on the elk-birthing corridor. Next the trail comes to, and continues along, an old jeep road that has an aggressive grade. This road has several switchbacks and leads to the top of Lionshead Rock. There are three overlooks along the way, each with increasingly good views of the valley and the surrounding mountains and meadows. The area at the top of Lionshead Rock is perfect for a picnic lunch. Retrace your steps to return.

An Optional Route: Folks can access Lionshead Rock by using the Vail gondola—and lift-served area of Vail—to gain elevation. Then, they leave the ski area and travel along Cougar Ridge for several miles and then descend to Lionshead Rock. This is a popular and aggressive summer bike trail or a long hike (see Vail Mountain options).

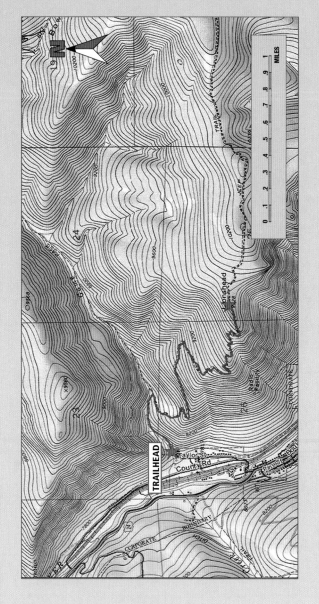

8. Lonesome Lake

BY CAROL GLASSON

MAPS	Trails Illustrated, Holy Cross/ Ruedi Reservoir, Number 126 Latitude 40, Vail & Eagle Trails
ELEVATION GAIN	1,560 feet
RATING	Moderate
ROUND-TRIP DISTANCE	10.4 miles
ROUND-TRIP TIME	5–6 hours
NEAREST LANDMARK	Town of Red Cliff

COMMENT: Except for the length, this trail is an easy gem, with gentle grades most of the way. The reward is an isolated glacial lake, nestled within the primitive Holy Cross Wilderness Area. The 122,797-acre expanse was designated as a wilderness area in 1980 and has 164 trails.

This particular wilderness takes its name from the 14,005-foot Mount of the Holy Cross, but the area boasts more than 25 peaks over 13,000 feet in elevation. Holy Cross represents the archetypal Colorado wilderness area. These soaring ridges and peaks, composed of 1.7 billion-year-old schist and gneiss, tower over immense U-shaped, glacial-carved valleys whose headwaters contain placid emerald lakes. Lonesome Lake is a wonderful example of these.

At the trailhead, you'll see the 45,000 acre-foot Homestake Reservoir. Although 97 percent of the water arrives from May through July, the reservoir delivers this precious resource to surrounding communities year round. The Homestake trans-mountain diversion system collects water from several tributaries of Homestake Creek and stores the water in Homestake Reservoir. It then delivers the water through the 5.2 mile-long Homestake Tunnel—going under

The emerald green of Lonesome Lake, and the ridge at 12,700 feet.

PHOTO BY CAROL GLASSON

the Continental Divide—and finally into Turquoise Reservoir, near Leadville.

GETTING THERE: Travel on I-70 from Vail to Exit 171, then travel south on US 24 through Minturn and Red Cliff. After you have traveled 13 miles, you will see Homestake Road, No. 703, on your right, at a sharp turn in the highway. Proceed down Homestake Road for 10.5 miles. This is a well-traveled gravel road and can get very dusty and "wash boardy." Continue past the Gold Park Campground to the small parking area on the right, across from the trailhead and just before a road intersection leading to the reservoir's dam 0.5 miles beyond.

THE ROUTE: From the trailhead, at 10,005 feet, the first 0.75 mile of the trail climbs through the forest and opens into the first of two large meadows. Look for some old cabin s across the meadow to the left. The grade mellows ˛ skirts just above the meadow, with intermittent views ᴊf beaver ponds and the creek below as you stretch your legs for about a mile.

As you re-enter the woods, the grades become a bit steeper. Cross a creek and enter a second meadow filled with wild-flowers. Watch for indian paintbrush, aster, and the small elephant head—a fuchsia-colored, clustered flower in the shape of an elephant's head. In this area, you'll see evidence of past avalanches coursing from the chutes above. The trail then re-enters the woods and begins a steady climb toward the lake.

Once you've reached an open basin surrounded by mountain peaks, turn around and see the view behind you back down the valley of East Fork Homestake Creek. (*Side note*: at approximately 3.5 miles, Isolation Creek will come in from the left [east]. Look for the faint trail following the water and leading up to Isolation Lakes. The last 0.5 mile is totally without trail, but the reward is a beautiful alpine lake guarded by Galena Mountain, 12,893 feet.)

As you continue on toward Lonesome Lake, keep to the far left for the last 0.5-mile climb to the grass-covered bench/shelf and the lake. This cirque lake is nestled in the mountain-walled glacial valley and can't be missed. If you enjoy fishing, you can find sucker, channel catfish, and crappie in the lake. The trail can be faint, especially in spring, so note where you traveled for your return to the trailhead.

IN WINTER: Ski touring and snowshoeing options—from Homestake Road, continue on Hwy 24, south, to the Cooper Ski Area. Across the road are a parking lot and toilets. There are a variety of signed trails here—from a short, 2.0 mile route to the longer Mitchell Creek Loop at approximately 7 miles. Portions of these trails follow the Colorado Trail. (Refer to the Trails Illustrated, Breckenridge/Tennessee Pass map, No. 109.)

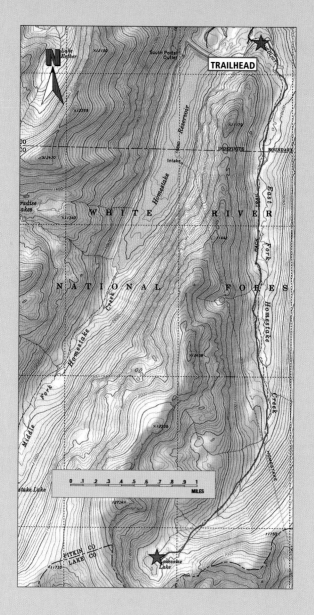

LONESOME LAKE   51

9. Mayflower Gulch

BY JAN DUDLEY

MAPS	Trails Illustrated, Breckenridge/Tennessee Pass, Number 109 Summit, Vail & Holy Cross Sky Terrain Trail Map
ELEVATION GAIN	About 700 feet
RATING	Easy
ROUND-TRIP DISTANCE	4+ miles in winter; longer in summer
ROUND-TRIP TIME	2 hours
NEAREST LANDMARK	5.7 miles south of Copper Mountain Ski Area, on Hwy 91

COMMENT: The stellar scenery and historic reminders of the region's mining activity combine to make this a popular Vail area destination. Pacific Peak, the easily recognizable "shark's tooth" along the Tenmile Range, helps to form the Mayflower Amphitheatre and is easily recognizable as you crest Vail Pass from the west.

The ease of access and a relatively easy ascent make Mayflower Gulch Trail appealing to local recreationists and visitors. This area is a popular destination in all seasons, because it offers snowshoers, cross-country skiers, hikers, and mountain bikers an opportunity to enjoy beautiful scenery with relatively light effort. From about mid-June through late July, the scenic reward includes sub-alpine wildflowers. In fall, golden aspen enhance the beautiful views. In winter, the trailhead bustles with cross-country skiers and back-country alpine touring or telemark skiers who "skin up" for turns on the Gold Hill shoulder. In addition to spectacular views, the area is used for geocaching activities, as well as

An old cabin's window nicely frames Jaques Peak to the west.

PHOTO BY FRANK BURZYNSKI

access to the ruins of the Boston Mine—considered by *Backpacker Magazine* as one of the "Top 3 Ghost Town Hikes" (June 2010). Rock hounds may still search the area for gems. The trailhead can also be the starting point for ascents of the surrounding "13-ers" (peaks over 13,000 feet elevation) in the Tenmile Range. Surrounding high 13-ers include Pacific Peak (13,950 feet), Crystal Peak (13,852 feet), and Fletcher Mountain (13,951 feet). Some hikers even go as far as Quandary Peak (14,265 feet). In all seasons, expect to encounter a wide range of trail users, often accompanied by dogs.

GETTING THERE: Access the trailhead from CO 91, on the "Top of the Rockies Scenic Byway." From I-70, Exit 195, drive south, past the stoplight at Copper Mountain, 5.7 miles toward Leadville. There are no signs on the highway indicating the trailhead, so watch carefully and turn left into the large parking area, before reaching the summit of Freemont Pass. There are no restroom facilities at the trailhead.

THE ROUTE: This trail description is based on winter travel. There is an average grade of 7 percent and, in winter, you can go 2 miles or more uphill, depending upon your ambition and careful consideration of avalanche risk. Avalanche hazard on the trail portion in the valley is low; it should be factored in for travel beyond the valley. In the summer hikers may travel farther on this trail, or connect to associated trails in adjacent basins, but such extensions are not considered in this trail description.

From the parking lot, at 11,000 feet, the trail ascends the gulch/basin along the south side of Mayflower Creek, and across the wetlands of Mayflower Hill (12,389 feet). Go up past an early left fork, stay right and enter into a pleasant trail/lane. This way is lined with Douglas fir and spruce trees and offers a pleasant reprieve from the pine bark beetle devastation elsewhere in the region. Look for an ore chute to the right of the trail, at just less than 1.0 mile.

The trail stays sheltered in the trees for about 1.4 miles, then opens into the Mayflower Amphitheatre and spectacular views of surrounding peaks—Pacific Peak at 13,950 feet and Fletcher Mountain at 13,951 feet.

The left fork, mentioned above, leads past a gate, past the obvious remains of three mining cabins and, beyond and higher up, toward the Boston Mine. Ascend as desired and as conditions allow. Winter backcountry ski tracks may be seen on the slopes of Gold Hill, to the west. Return the same way you came up.

Adventurous and experienced summer hikers may want to return to the trailhead by ascending Gold Hill and looping back. Be sure to consult with one of the listed map sources before attempting this route.

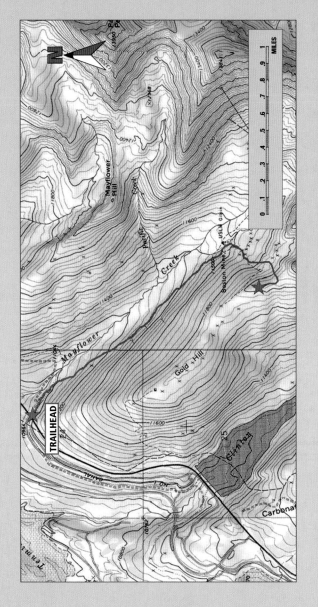

MILES

N

Mayflower Hill

Pacific Creek

Mayflower Creek

Boston Mine

USL Claim

Gold Hill

Gitschen

TRAILHEAD

CANAL

Carbonat

10. Missouri Pass/Fancy Pass

BY HAP YOUNG

MAPS	Trails Illustrated Holy Cross/ Ruedi Reservoir, Number 126
	USGS, Mount of the Holy Cross/Mount Jackson, 7.5 minute
	Sky Terrain maps—Summit, Vail, & Holy Cross Latitude 40, Vail & Eagle Trails
ELEVATION GAIN	2,620 feet
RATING	Moderate–difficult
ROUND-TRIP DISTANCE	10 miles
ROUND-TRIP TIME	8–9 hours
NEAREST LANDMARK	Town of Redcliff

COMMENT: On this hike you will experience woods, open meadows, wildflowers, grand rock formations, cascading waterfalls, sparkling lakes above timberline, mountain passes with snowfields, and "forever" views. It's best to hike this loop in July/August. The trail is well-traveled but it's still a good idea to bring your hiking poles, because you may have to cross a few snowfields when approaching higher elevations. Anticipate a profusion of alpine flowers growing in rock crevices and near the snowmelt runoff.

Note: If you prefer a more moderate 4- to 5-hour round-trip excursion, hike from the parking area to either Fancy Lake (2.4 miles one way/elevation gain of 1,160 feet) or Lower Missouri Lake (3.6 miles one way/elevation gain of 1,280 feet), have lunch, enjoy the scenery, and return the same way you hiked up. In either case, you will be at treeline with awesome views of sheer rock rising to the ridgeline peaks.

Missouri Lakes from the pass above.   PHOTO BY GENE MARSH

GETTING THERE: From Vail, drive west on I-70 to Exit 171 and take US 24 south (through Minturn) for 12.2 miles and turn right onto Homestake Road (CR# 703). Drive 7.9 miles (passing Gold Park Campground on your left) to a right turn on CR 704. On 704, drive another 2.1 miles to trailhead parking. Facing the two trailhead signs, Missouri Lakes Trailhead is to your left and Fancy Lake Trailhead is 50 yards to the right.

THE ROUTE: (This description is for a clockwise loop starting at the Missouri Lakes Trailhead.) Start your walk on an old jeep trail and go 0.5 mile to the trail sign: "Entering the Holy Cross Wilderness." The footpath is well-traveled so it is easy to follow to Lower Missouri Lake. In the first 2.0 miles, bridges crisscross the creek. Next are a few short and steeper sections—look for the dramatic stair-step waterfall, and from above view the narrow cut the water has made through the granite. Eventually Missouri Creek slows down and opens up to a beautiful meadow and small pond. The next

1.6 miles take you through a wooded area before coming to a marsh with several short boardwalks to keep your feet dry.

The horizon starts to open up and magnificent Savage Peak (13,139 feet) looms large to your left (south). Continue up a final steep pitch, level off, and Lower Missouri Lake (11,400 feet) will appear below a gigantic rock cirque.

To continue on to Upper Missouri Lake (11,502 feet) and Missouri Pass (11,986 feet), take the trail to your right (north). You will pass some smaller ponds and in less than 0.3 mile you will arrive at the plateau for the largest lake, Upper Missouri Lake. Hike another 0.5 mile to the pass—you will traverse some switchbacks for the final 300 yards (and maybe a few snowfields)—to reach the saddle of Missouri Pass. Sweeping views look west into the Cross Creek Valley and, to the far north, Mount Jackson (13,670 feet).

The trail from Missouri Pass to Fancy Pass is about 1.5 miles. Hike north off the pass and, at the trail sign near Treasure Vault Lake, take the right fork, going north toward Fancy Pass (12,380 feet). (The left fork goes down into Cross Creek Drainage.) Your final 400 yards will go right (east) to the saddle.

On Fancy Pass, you have another spectacular panorama, with Treasure Vault and Blodgett Lake behind you to the west/southwest. This saddle is actually part of the Holy Cross Ridge, although you are quite a distance from its summit.

Start your descent staying left (keeping the steep talus gully on your left), because the trail may be out of sight if covered by snow and not packed down. This longer, steep section eventually merges onto an old wagon road (which continues to Holy Cross City). When Fancy Lake comes into view, look for one of the short gullies on your right and drop down to the lake. For your hike down from Fancy Lake, follow the creek outflow (on your right) and the foot trail will appear within 100 yards. In another 2.4 miles you will arrive at the trailhead parking area and your car.

TRAILHEAD

MILES

MISSOURI LAKES

Fancy Pass

Missouri Creek

Fancy Creek

Holy Cross City

STATION

Cleveland Rock

Homestake Creek

11. Mount Thomas

BY JUDITH RAU

MAPS	Trails Illustrated Holy Cross Ruedi Reservoir, Number 126 Latitude 40, Vail & Eagle Trails
ELEVATION GAIN	2,459 feet
RATING	Moderate–difficult
ROUND-TRIP DISTANCE	9.5 miles
ROUND-TRIP TIME	6–7 hours
NEAREST LANDMARK	Sylvan Lake State Park

COMMENT: Mount Thomas, at just less than 12,000 feet, is unsurpassed in Eagle County for its spectacular and expansive views. On a clear day you can see, way up to the northeast, Rocky Mountain National Park; due north to the Flat Tops; and the Elks to the southwest. You'll also see the northern end of the Sawatch Range with the jagged summits of Fools Peak, Eagle Peak, and Avalanche Peak just across the valley and to the east of where the trail starts.

Mount Thomas' red sandstone formation sets it apart from all the local granite mountains and adds to its wonderful hiking experience. Mount Thomas is part of the long ridge called Red Table Mountain, a unique mountain range that trends east to west for 20 miles and consists of maroon sandstone, a sedimentary sandstone layer left over from the inland sea that covered this area millions of years ago.

GETTING THERE: From Vail, drive west on I-70 to Exit 147. Head south on Eby Creek Road across the Eagle River. Enter the round-about and go west on Hwy 6 and quickly turn left on Capital Street. Start your mileage count here. Go through

Fools, Eagle, and Avalanche Peaks, to the east.   PHOTO BY JUDITH RAU

town for 0.8 mile and turn left at the stop, on to Brush Creek Road. Follow the signs to Sylvan Lake State Park. Shortly past the visitors' center, at mile 15.3, stay right at the Y. (The road now changes from paved to improved gravel.) Continue past Sylvan Lake, where the road becomes rougher—it is still navigable in most passenger cars so long as the surface is dry.

At mile 16.3, stay left to Crooked Creek Pass, FR 400. At mile 20.7, you are on top of the pass, at 10,000 feet. Cross the cattle guard and park on the right, along the road. Hike slightly downward along this road, 0.25 mile, past a large campsite on the left, and now upward to where the road takes a sharp right turn. Continue up the road; stay left at a Y and again immediately at another Y, and head back to the south side of the ridge, for a total of about 1.25 miles. You will arrive at a high-tension power line.

This power line/utility road continues on back down and into the next valley, but the trailhead is located here, right under the power line, where the road crests the shoulder of the mountain. As of this writing, the trailhead sign is missing.

THE ROUTE: Starting at 10,500 feet, this is a well-defined trail heading southwest into the conifer forest. From this point you

Parry's bellflower against the red sandstone of Red Table Mountain.
PHOTO BY JUDITH RAU

have views down into the Hunter-Fryingpan Wilderness. The trail climbs up and around the steep face to the first ridge, in long, easy switchbacks. The forest intermittently opens up to wildflower-studded meadows, where you are treated to wonderful views of the mountains to the south. After a few short and steep switchbacks, at about 1.5 miles, you end up on top of the first ridge; there's a slight summit at 11,602 feet. From here, you can see down onto Sylvan Lake and beyond to the Flat Tops.

The trail continues along this ridge, through forest at a gentle downhill slope, losing about 200 feet of elevation and ending at a short knife-edge. It then starts climbing, quite steeply and somewhat exposed, to the next broad ridge, which features open meadows of tundra with 360-degree views. Very visible red rock cairns show the way along this gentle stretch of trail. It then starts climbing again, this time along and up the red, scree-covered south face of the actual Mount Thomas.

As soon as the trail tops out on the ridge again, leave it (the trail continues along Red Table Mountain all the way to Cottonwood Pass), do a 90-degree turn right, and walk about 100 yards up the gentle grassy slope to the summit, marked by a large rock cairn. Retrace your steps for the hike back to the trailhead.

TRAILHEAD

MILES

12. New York Mountain

BY JUDITH RAU

MAPS	Trails Illustrated, Eagle/Avalon, Number 121
ELEVATION GAIN	1,350 feet
RATING	Moderate
ROUND-TRIP DISTANCE	4 miles
ROUND-TRIP TIME	3–4 hours
NEAREST LANDMARK	Historic town of Fulford

COMMENT: You'd like to hike one of the higher peaks in Colorado and enjoy the majestic views of the wild crags of the Holy Cross Wilderness Area. However, you're reluctant to tackle a long, steep, and difficult hike. New York Mountain would be a good option for you.

It's possible to drive almost any car with all-wheel-drive and moderate clearance to the trailhead, at 11,200 feet. The hike from there will take you to the top of the world in about 1.5 to 2.0 hours. You'll be able to see mountains as far away as the Elk Range to the west; many of the highest peaks in the Eagles Nest Wilderness Area to the north and east; and Mount Jackson and Gold Dust Peak nearby.

Along the way, you'll be able to explore Colorado's mining history while passing the abandoned Polar Star Mine and a number of smaller mining remnants. To be safe and to respect private property, please stay out of all mines. The historic town of Fulford is also worth visiting. Once a thriving mining town, it is now a scattering of mostly new, and some not so new, second homes. One or two permanent residents rely upon snowmobiles to get around in winter.

New York Mountain is also a favorite of backcountry skiers and snowshoers, because the Tenth Mountain Polar Star hut

Looking south along the summit ridge.   PHOTO BY JUDITH RAU

and yurt are located near the New York Mountain Trailhead. Access in winter, however, is a bit more difficult and these folks must start their trek at Yeoman Park.

GETTING THERE: From Vail, travel west on I-70 and take Eagle Exit 147. Turn left over the highway, on Eby Creek Road, traveling to Hwy 6. Go west at the roundabout and take the first left onto Capitol Street. Continue through town for 0.8 mile and, at a three-way stop, turn left onto Brush Creek Road. From here, follow signs to Sylvan Lake State Park. Continue past the visitors' center; at mile 15.3, there will be a Y. Take the left fork onto FS Rd 415. The road is now improved gravel. Continue past Yeoman Park and, at mile 16, take a left onto FS Rd 418 toward Fulford. Pass the entrance to Fulford at mile 19.7 and continue on the main road. After crossing the cattle guard, at 21.4 miles, stay on FS Rd 418 on the right. The road becomes rougher, but all-wheel-drive will be sufficient. Keep left at mile 24.6 to parking and the trailhead, at 25.3 miles.

The many alpine wildflowers, on the northern shoulder of New York Mountain.   PHOTO BY JUDITH RAU

THE ROUTE: The well-signed New York Mountain Trail, FS 1878, starts here, crossing the historic Polar Star Mine site. At the first switchback, the old mining road becomes a moderately steep trail as it climbs through old growth conifer forest and a variety of wildflowers. When the forest ends at tree line and you enter into the high alpine meadow, a sign will indicate that you are entering Holy Cross Wilderness Area and to take the trail to the right to New York Mountain.

Head south up and over the extensive scree field at a moderate climb—well-placed stone cairns and an occasional old wooden post will show the way. As you reach the saddle between the two prominent summit peaks, head up the less defined trail, skirting around another abandoned mine site. The summit to your left (north) is the higher of the two (12,550 vs. 12,475 feet), but if you feel ambitious claim them both.

Note: the more prominent trail heading across the saddle leads down to Nolan Lake. Following that trail makes this a "thru-hike," several more miles and requiring a second vehicle. The trail to Nolan Lake comes up from the town of Fulford, about 5 miles and 2,200 feet below.

The easier way back is to return the way you came. Pay attention and use the right trail once you are back in the forest and almost down, because there is a trail coming up from the Polar Star hut and yurts. If you miss this, as I have done, just follow the road out—it eventually leads to the parking area.

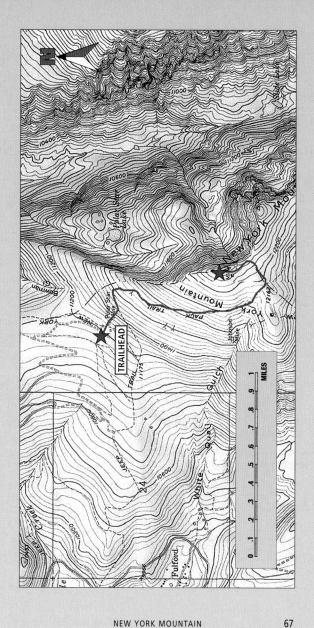

NEW YORK MOUNTAIN

13. North Trail (Section 4: Son of Middle Creek to Red Sandstone)

BY AMY RIDGE

MAPS	Trails Illustrated, Vail/Frisco/Dillon, Number 108 Latitude 40, Vail & Eagle Trails *(See Addendum to Maps)
ELEVATION GAIN	1,150 feet
RATING	Moderate
ROUND-TRIP DISTANCE	3.9 miles
ROUND-TRIP TIME	2.5 hours
NEAREST LANDMARK	Town of Vail

COMMENT: The entire North Trail, 12.15 miles, meanders along the north side of our narrow valley. It is across from Vail Ski Area and affords stunning views of the town, the ski runs, and the distant peaks. The trail's sections of single track extend through aspen and pines, from a trailhead west of I-70's Exit 173 to the trailhead for this hike, just off I-70's Exit 176.

This easternmost section—our favorite—is a worthy introduction to the North Trail and will likely tempt you to return. This is a multi-use trail and you may see bikers, horses, and dogs on leashes (as required).

From April 15 to July 1, the trail is closed to all usages to protect newborn wildlife and to mitigate erosion during the spring runoff.

Our route is described from east to west (although either way works). If you have limited time, we recommend using a shuttle vehicle. This will also prevent you from having to walk back on pavement, as a "loop hike." Alternately, you

Vail Ski Mountain and Village. PHOTO BY AMY RIDGE

can go as far as you wish on the trail, one-way, and return to your starting point.

GETTING THERE: To drop a shuttle vehicle, go to the top of the traffic circle on the north side of I-70's Exit 176 (the main Vail exit) and continue west on the north frontage road, which parallels I-70. In 0.9 mile, turn right onto Red Sandstone Road, which is the first real street you encounter after passing several driveways and bus stops.

After less than 0.3 mile, there is a right switchback, where you will see a small parking area. You might stop here and study the poster-board map of the entire North Trail. This point is the trailhead for the next section, west of the hike described here. Our hike is between points A4 and A5 on this map.

Continue on Red Sandstone Road, make the left switchback, and at the top of the incline, go straight onto a dirt road—do *not* switchback right. This is Piney Lake Road. Reset your odometer and go 0.5 mile to a small parking area on your right, with an information board straight ahead. Leave a shuttle vehicle here (or start hiking, because this trail can easily be done in either direction). The actual trail is visible back down the road a short distance and marked with a trailhead sign.

Retrace your drive back to the traffic circle at Exit 176, go almost entirely around it, but stop at the top and turn right, onto Spraddle Creek Road. The trailhead for our hike is in the unsigned parking lot immediately to the northeast of the roundabout.

THE ROUTE: From the North Trail sign at the end of the parking lot, head out along the obvious path. At first, the tall grass, wildflowers, and aspen may obscure your view across the switchbacks that await you, so be aware of mountain bikers who could suddenly appear.

Watch the valley open up, and I-70 recede, as you start to climb. After about 20 minutes, larger aspens and large evergreens provide shade and I-70 is gone. Another 20 minutes later you'll cross a well-made footbridge over Middle Creek. Currently there is a signpost marking this junction. Take a rest here and prepare for a fairly steep 20-minute climb and a 500-foot elevation gain. Once you complete the climb you are at the top (9,400 feet), where the Son of Middle Creek Trail comes in on your right. You've hiked 1.6 miles up and have another 2.3 miles to go—all downhill. Stop to enjoy the views from this high vantage point.

Continue ahead and slightly to the right on a tree-lined trail that will switchback repeatedly as you descend. As you approach the southern corners of the switchbacks, you'll have great views of the town, the ski slopes, and the mountain background. Look for Mount of the Holy Cross in the distance and the aptly named Notch Mountain to its left.

A final switchback will lead you to a lengthy stand of aspen that opens up to a clearing for power lines. After passing under the power lines, you reenter the aspens, by some stacked logs, and continue your switchback descent. Soon you exit onto Piney Lake Road, where your vehicle awaits.

This section is just one of North Trail's four sections, but definitely our favorite.

---

*Addendum to Maps. You may want to review: White River National Forest, Eagle/ Holy Cross Recreation Quicksheet, North Trail #1896—Red Sandstone to Son of Middle Creek. (Quicksheet maps are on the Internet and also available at the Holy Cross Ranger District Office, 970-827-5715. Exit I-70 at the Minturn Exit, turn right and the office is the next right.)

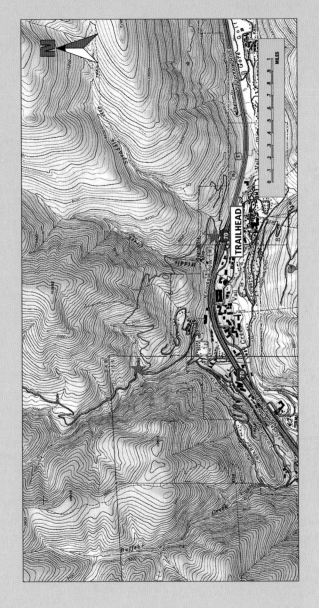

14. Notch Mountain

BY CHARLIE CARTER

MAPS	USGS, Mount of the Holy Cross, 7.5 minute Latitude 40, Vail & Eagle Trails
ELEVATION GAIN	2,760 feet
RATING	Moderate–difficult
ROUND-TRIP DISTANCE	8 miles
ROUND-TRIP TIME	7 hours
NEAREST LANDMARK	I-70, Exit 171

COMMENT: While this outing is named Notch Mountain, the hike actually terminates at the 13,080-foot Stone Shelter, not the twin summits forming the distinctive notch. The shelter sits 0.25 miles to the south of the summit, on a high ridge. Notch Mountain, conspicuously visible from Hwy 24 south of Minturn, sits due east of the famous Mount of the Holy Cross. It is separated from that mountain by a chasm that is 1.0 mile wide and 1,000 feet deep. The legendary view of Holy Cross was first photographed in 1873, by William Henry Jackson.

You can experience this view personally by making the long climb up the relatively easy east ridge of Notch Mountain. The trail gently climbs 2,760 feet, thanks to switchbacks thoughtfully engineered into the trail. Progress will be steady and the trail rarely seems truly steep. Soon you will be well up on the mountain, enjoying the feeling of climbing above timberline, and seeing the forest slowly disappear—replaced by shorter trees, shrubs, and fields of wildflowers.

GETTING THERE: Start on Exit 171 on I-70, three miles west of Vail. Follow the signs on Hwy 24 to Minturn/Leadville and drive south through Minturn. At 4.7 miles from I-70, locate

Mount of the Holy Cross and climber's cabin, as seen from the summit of Notch Mountain. PHOTO BY SCOTT MCCLARRINON

the small sign pointing to the right (west) for National Forest Tigiwon Road access. This dirt road can be driven, carefully, in a sedan and winds uphill through forest for eight miles to the USFS Halfmoon Campground. Allow one hour driving time from I-70. Weekend parking may be tight. There are two trailheads, with separate signage.

THE ROUTE: Identify the sign for Lake Constantine/Fall Creek/ Notch Mountain. It is to the left as you face south, slightly lower than its counterpart. Start slowly on the wide, gentle trail in the deep forest—you will soon confront a challenge and will need your reserves. Hike deliberately and carefully along some exposed areas where the mountain has seen periodic massive rockslides.

After 2.25 miles, and an hour plus of pleasant hiking, you will come to the signed turnoff to Notch Mountain to the right. (The trail straight ahead leads to Lake Constantine.) Enjoy a break—your real work is about to begin.

Follow the excellent trail as it slowly leaves the forest and heads unrelentingly toward the summit. To the left, you will soon encounter the first of 41 switchbacks. Several more switchbacks will bring you into endless meadows of wildflowers. Look north to see the famous Back Bowls of the Vail Ski Area, backstopped by the Gore Range. Next, the left side of the

Looking northeast toward the Gore Range. PHOTO BY GRACE WELLWERTS

notch will come into view. A switchback to the north allows you to peer down into the rough and severe gully that, at the top, separates the two notches. A switchback to the south provides views of three small and pristine alpine lakes.

The switchbacks come closer together now as you see only rocks and occasional displays of wildflowers. *Please,* do not take shortcuts across the switchbacks, even if you see other hikers doing it. Shortcuts won't save you any time but they can destroy some of the trails' support and harm the fragile tundra.

A final switchback to the left will tease you with views of summits and then the monarch itself—Mount of the Holy Cross—will appear. The view is both overpowering and inspirational. A partial collapse of the right arm of the cross is the only change since the famous 1873 photo.

The stone shelter will be open but, please, leave no initials, graffiti, or trash. Enjoy the view and a leisurely lunch break. From the turnoff at the bottom, you will need about three hours to make the 2.0-mile climb. This will allow you time for taking pictures, studying the wildflowers, and just taking it all in. Be prepared for some wind and surprisingly cool temperatures.

The descent to the trail junction can be done in about two hours, and then maybe another hour back to the trailhead. Keep your eyes on the trail to avoid stumbling and be glad you brought your hiking poles along.

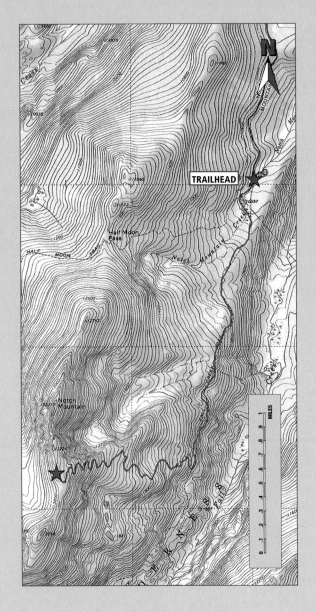

TRAILHEAD

15. Seven Sisters Lakes/Fall Creek Pass/Whitney Peak

BY CHARLIE CARTER

MAPS	USGS, Mount of the Holy Cross, 7.5 minute Latitude 40, Vail & Eagle Trails
ELEVATION GAIN	2,990 feet (to Peak summit)
RATING	Moderate–difficult
ROUND-TRIP DISTANCE	9 miles
ROUND-TRIP TIME	9 hours
NEAREST LANDMARK	I-70, Exit 171

COMMENT: This hike takes you into a spectacular valley surrounded by tall peaks dotted with snowfields. These snowfields drain into a chain of lakes, all connected by streams and meadows sprouting wildflowers. A decent trail connects all of this beauty.

You may visit just the lakes or hike past them up to Fall Creek Pass, at the head of the valley and above timberline. If you want more, add the easy ascent of Whitney Peak—your pace, conditioning, available time, and weather will help you with this decision.

Unfortunately, the approach to this wonderful alpine world involves some extra driving, walking up an unpleasant four-wheel-drive road, and the annual washout threats to the approach roads. This hike, however, is worth it. Entering the Holy Cross Wilderness Area soon puts all this behind you. Sedans can handle the drive.

GETTING THERE: Start on Exit 171 on I-70, 3 miles west of Vail. Follow the signs on Hwy 24 to Minturn/Leadville and drive

Viewing the upper lakes after coming back from Fall Creek Pass.
PHOTO BY NATHAN FREE

south through Minturn. At about 13 miles from I-70, make a sharp right turn onto dirt Homestake Road (USFS 703). Just past the Gold Park Campground, about 8 miles in, turn right on USFS 704 heading to Missouri Lakes Trailhead. Drive 2 more miles uphill, to the trailhead, and turn sharply north onto an unmarked dirt road. Go 2 miles, heading back toward French Creek and the Holy Cross City four-wheel-drive road. Park at the wide spot below the Diversion Dam shown on the map.

THE ROUTE: Walk a short distance to the Holy Cross City four-wheel-drive road and turn left up its steep course. Note: you may encounter some serious four-wheel-drive "jeepers" on the road. At about 1.25 miles, just past an ugly stream crossing, look for the hiking trail veering off to the right, marked by a fence structure, and leave the jeep road. The valley opens up now and curves to the right. Shortly, pass to the right of Hunky Dory Lake. You are now in wilderness. This good trail continues straight and fairly steeply for about 0.50 mile, up to about 11,700 feet elevation, where it curves right and levels off. The lakes will begin to pass in review and wildflowers abound. Hidden waterfalls reward the careful observer.

At about 2.5 miles, skip across small rocks in a connecting stream. Consider this site for an extended break. Whitney Peak looms above you to the right. The trail is occasionally overgrown, but won't hide from you for long. A massive wall soon faces you and the now sketchy trail ascends the right side. Turn around here and memorize your return route. Continue on the trail above timberline, and admire the lakes, meadows, and wildflowers. The valley now narrows as you approach the snowfields below 12,600-foot Fall Creek Pass. Climb on and, at about the 3.5-mile mark, you will reach the summit of the pass. The craggy southern extension of the Holy Cross Ridge is to your left—north.

You have now climbed 2,320 feet from the 10,280-foot trailhead. Whitney Peak, to the south, requires 670 feet more of climbing. If you are up for this, scramble due south for about 10 minutes, through some high rocks. Then continue southeast, up the gentle slope toward the skyline. Your route steepens slightly; keep to the left of a small headwall and look for grassy benches, which indicate relatively gentle terrain. Step lightly on the fragile tundra; durable rocks are better. The slope soon eases onto a moon-like landscape, interspersed with grass. Arrive on the rounded summit in less than an hour. Look for the single monolith rock, with its USGS Survey plaque indicating the true summit.

Note your landmarks to the north as you ascend, especially if the weather is threatening. Expect wind and temperatures in the 50- to 60-degree range during the summer. Looking west, enjoy the views of the Aspen area's 14,000-foot peaks—from left to right: Pyramid, the Maroon Bells, Snowmass, and Capitol. Note the highest of the Seven Sisters Lakes behind you, situated at 12,750 feet and likely still frozen.

Your descent will require three to four hours. The downhill slope warrants constant attention to avoid tripping and slipping on the many small stones on the trail—hiking poles are helpful.

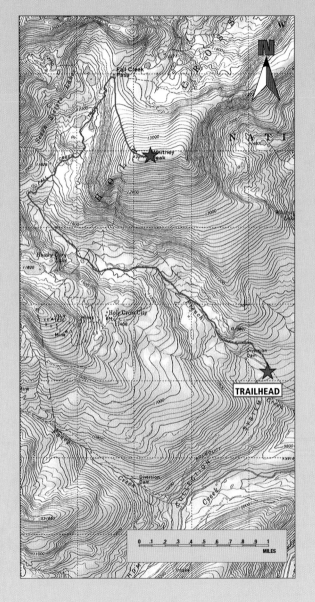

16. Shrine Ridge and Holy Cross Overlook

BY RITA THOMPSON

MAPS	Trails Illustrated, Vail/Frisco/ Dillon, Number 108 USGS Vail Pass, Red Cliff Trails, 7.5 minute
ELEVATION GAIN	874 feet
RATING	Easy
ROUND-TRIP DISTANCE	4.2 miles
ROUND-TRIP TIME	3–4 hours
NEAREST LANDMARK	Vail Pass

COMMENT: The eastern flank and meadows off Shrine Ridge and nearby Wilder Gulch are known to have some of the best indian paintbrush, and other wildflowers, in Colorado. Ideal as an introduction to hiking in the mountains, Shrine Mountain has the novelty of almost always having some snow on or near the trail and has spectacular 360-degree views once you are on the ridge.

The name Shrine Ridge was coined by early settlers who considered it a great spot, or "shrine," for viewing "God's Holy Cross."

People may also enjoy this trail in the winter while visiting the nearby 10th Mountain Division Huts (available to rent through 10th Mountain Division Hut Association). Shrine Pass is not plowed in the winter, so access is only available from Vail Pass Rest Area.

GETTING THERE: From the main Vail roundabout, drive east on I-70. At 14.5 miles, take Exit 190/Vail Pass Rest Area (15 minutes drive time). Restrooms are available on the loop

The beautiful alpine flowers at the "shrine" to Mount of the Holy Cross. PHOTO BY SELMA KRISTEL

through the rest area. Take the fork to the right (dirt road) onto the Shrine Pass, Red Cliff FDR # 709. At the next fork, stay left, on the main road. At 2.4 miles from I-70 (10 minutes), turn left into the Shrine Ridge Trailhead parking lot (equipped with chemical toilets).

THE ROUTE: From the parking lot (elevation 11,089 feet), walk up the dirt driveway to the south and, just before the gate leading to Shrine Mountain Inn cabins, turn left at the sign indicating Shrine Ridge Trailhead. Hike slightly downhill through meadows and wetlands and past beaver ponds, and gradually and steadily go up through the lodgepole pine forest. You will have to maneuver gushing streams in the spring and early summer; they will become tiny trickles later on.

At the junction sign, Shrine Mountain Inn, follow Shrine Ridge Trail #2016 up to the left. Where the forest thins out (11,500 feet), there's a steep rock outcropping and the trail veers toward and through the rocks on the right. Below, there's a huge flat rock, perfect for sunning.

After clearing the rocks, follow the path straight up, and you will see, or have to walk across, snow left over from the previous winter. Just a few feet uphill from the snow, on the left, there's a marker with a blue diamond (11,755 feet). You are now on the broad, flat ridge. Take the gradual trail to the right, with views of the chimney rocks, and stay high on the main trail. On the high rocks, look for the US Geological Survey marker on the top of Shrine Mountain (elevation 11,888 feet). Above and behind the chimney rocks to the north part of the Gore Range is in view, and Mount of the Holy Cross is due west.

Once on the Shrine Ridge, you can easily explore the relatively flat—100-foot elevation gain—0.2-mile route along the ridge to the south, toward Copper Mountain and Wilder Gulch.

To return, simply reverse your route. At the arrow, take the trail to the east and, at the blue diamond sign, turn left to go back to the parking lot. Remember that there is a slight uphill finish to the trailhead.

An Optional Route: Mount of the Holy Cross Overlook (wheelchair accessible and only 0.5-mile round-trip.) Drive past the Shrine Ridge Trailhead parking lot and go west for another 1.4 miles on Shrine Pass Road, FDR#709, (10 minutes drive time), for a total 3.8 miles from I-70 (20 minutes). The parking lot is marked as "Mount of the Holy Cross Overlook." Park here for wheelchair access to the chemical toilet and trailhead (elevation 10,600 feet). It is 0.25 mile to the deck to view Mount of the Holy Cross (10 minutes).

There's a smooth and flat gravel pathway that goes through an open area, then slightly uphill through a lodgepole pine forest, and left up the ramp to secluded Julia's Deck. The view here is spectacular. This is also a nice location to view the mountains in the evening without getting caught on the trail after dark.

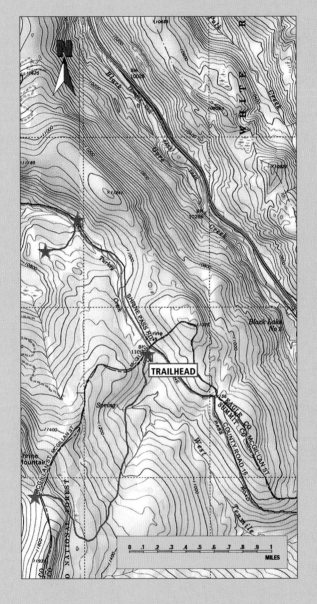

TRAILHEAD

17. Tuhare Lakes

BY CHARLIE CARTER

MAPS	USGS, Mount of the Holy Cross, 7.5 minute Latitude 40, Vail & Eagle Trails
ELEVATION GAIN	2,045 feet
RATING	Moderate–difficult
ROUND-TRIP DISTANCE	10.5 miles
ROUND-TRIP TIME	8–9 hours
NEAREST LANDMARK	Town of Minturn

COMMENT: The two lovely Tuhare Lakes, at 12,090 feet and 12,365 feet respectively, sit hidden in a narrow valley surrounded by rock slabs reaching well over 13,000 feet. The lakes sit on rock shelves, above timberline, drained by waterfalls, and with their access guarded. Hikers must work hard to reach these two alpine gems. Numerous snowfields dot the jumbled landscape and feed the many streams and waterfalls. Wildflowers are abundant and the sound of cool running water is everywhere.

This is an all-day experience—as you approach the lakes, you will be moving very slowly through the rough terrain. Your efforts, however, will be rewarded by amazing alpine beauty.

GETTING THERE: Your trip starts at Exit 171 of I-70, three miles west of Vail. Follow the signs on Highway 24 to Minturn/Leadville, and drive south through Minturn. At 4.7 miles from I-70, a small sign points to the right (west) for National Forest Tigiwon Road. This dirt road, which can be driven in a sedan, winds uphill through forest for 8 miles, and ends at the USFS Halfmoon Campground. Allow one hour driving

Reflections on Lower Tuhare Lake.   PHOTO BY GENE MARSH

time from I-70. Weekend parking may be tight. There are two trailheads, with separate signage.

THE ROUTE: Identify the trail to Lake Constantine/Fall Creek/ Notch Mountain. It is to the left and lower as you face south. Start slowly on the wide gentle trail in deep forest. Hike deliberately and carefully along some exposed areas through massive rockslides.

After 2.25 miles of pleasant hiking, you will come to the signed turnoff to Notch Mountain. Enjoy a break, then continue straight ahead another 2 miles to Lake Constantine. The trail, which gently rolls up and down, is in forest. Pass pretty Lake Constantine (11,371 feet) to your left and continue another 0.5 mile to a trail junction. The sign points straight ahead to Tuhare Lakes.

The quality and consistency of the trail soon deteriorates. Take heart—you can do it! You will use your hands to pull yourself up some of the more difficult places, but only for short distances. Your reward will be a view of the waterfalls and water glissading over smooth rock. If you lose the trail among the overhanging willows, pause and look around carefully.

The trail then heads to the right, away from the waterfall, and emerges to the right of a fairly large and permanent snowfield. Resist the temptation to climb on this slippery, steep surface. Instead, carefully pick your way along the rocks on the right side, using your hands until you can skirt the top end of the snowfield. Turn left across the top of this gully and head through giant boulders, back toward the center of the main valley. You will soon come to an overlook and see the shimmering waters of Lower Tuhare Lake below. The hanging valley between the two lakes is an alpine paradise and you may wish to terminate your hike here.

To continue to the upper lake, descend from the boulders, generally to the right, and locate the sketchy trail closer to the lakeshore. Huge barriers of granite walls and boulders shield the upper lake. Climb carefully among them, and across several small streams. After ascending the prominent wall on its right side, work your way toward the middle and the outlet stream. Pass through an area of VW-sized boulders. Depending on the amount of snow from the previous winter, and the time of year, you may easily lose the poor trail as it disappears under snowfields and snow bridges. Thread your way along the outlet stream, crossing it if necessary. Be very wary of snow bridges, because their collapse could send you into the icy water below. Turn around often to admire the views and to mentally note the route you came up; doing so will make your descent easier.

You will soon cover the 0.25 mile to the upper lake and pop out above a small, gorgeous waterfall and pool and onto the dramatic and stark lakeshore, at 12,365 feet. This is a great lunch spot. Remember, you have a 5-mile/4-hour descent back to the trailhead. Leave this special place reluctantly, but carefully. Again, resist the temptation to slide down the big snowfield you passed coming up. Take your time as you downclimb on the rocks. Retrace your steps back to Lake Constantine and down the Fall Creek Trail to your car.

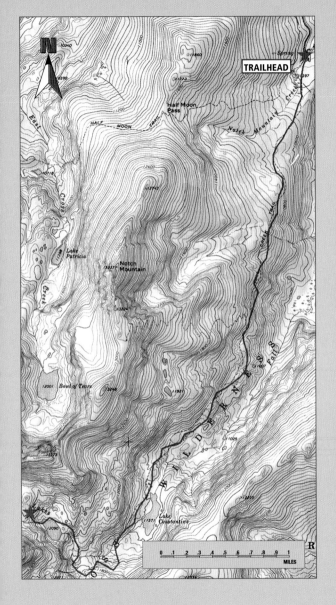

TUHARE LAKES 87

18. Uneva Peak

BY JIM CUNNINGHAM

MAPS	Trails Illustrated, Vail/Frisco/ Dillon, Number 108 Latitude 40, Vail & Eagle Trails
ELEVATION GAIN	1,912 feet
RATING	Moderate
ROUND-TRIP DISTANCE	5.75 miles
ROUND-TRIP TIME	3–5 hours
NEAREST LANDMARK	Vail Pass/I-70 and Vail Pass Rest Area

COMMENT: Uneva Peak offers a relatively easy way to summit a high peak with tremendous views. Beginning at Vail Pass, elevation 10,600 feet, this hike initially follows the route for the Corral Creek hike. Due to avalanche danger, Uneva Peak is NOT recommended as a winter trail.

GETTING THERE: The trailhead is simple to find, whether you are approaching from the east or west. Just take I-70 to the Vail Pass Rest Area. There is an upper and a lower parking lot in the rest area. The customary place to park is in the upper lot, but the area can become quite busy so you may want to park in the lower area, where the restrooms are located. The trailhead is located north, across I-70 and at the end of the overpass. The trail itself is marked with blue diamonds for directional reference.

THE ROUTE: (See the trail directions for Corral Creek.) Once you reach the top of the ridge on the Corral Creek hike (the northernmost point, where the creek begins), make a sharp right turn and head up into the trees. Your destination is the

The author enjoying some winter touring.   PHOTO BY JIM CUNNINGHAM

big open bowl below Uneva Peak, which is about 100 yards through the trees.

When you get into the trees, the loosely defined trail angles toward the right (east), through the trees to bring you out into the open bowl area. Be certain you are heading slightly right while in the woods. Once you are in the bowl, head straight up the middle of the bowl to the high point within the bowl. (Note there is no defined trail, so just make your way up the bowl to the high point.)

Once you are on this high point, look ahead and left (north) to see a faint trail angling left up the side of the hill to the top of the ridge. There may be a slight snowfield near the start of the trail, but continue straight ahead and the trail, angling left, will become apparent. Note that there are two trails, but the one you want is farther up in the bowl and does not cross the large talus field. Take this trail to the top of the ridge, where you will see a grove of evergreen trees. Keep walking and you will intersect a trail heading up the ridge.

Looking north to Red Buffalo Pass and the Gore Range, from the summit of Uneva.

PHOTO BY NATHAN FREE

Take a right turn and head up Uneva's west ridge toward the summit. The peak is not well defined from this direction, but maintain a heading up the ridge to the highest point in front of you and the summit will come into view. Once you are on the peak, you will have a tremendous view in all directions. This is one of the best spots to see Mount of the Holy Cross in the distance. You can also see most of the Gore Range, Copper Mountain Ski Area, Peaks 1–10, parts of the Flat Tops Wilderness Area, the back side of Vail Ski Resort (all the way to the top of Blue Sky Basin), and much more. Uneva Pass is visible just below you and to the southeast.

Note: From Uneva's southern ridge, it is rather easy to descend onto the Gore Range Trail (seen crossing Uneva Pass) and hike down to its trailhead in Frisco. Another option is to cross Uneva Pass and go on down to Copper Mountain. Both of these options will require car shuttles. Using a map, one can also follow Uneva's southern ridge down to a large burn area, and then head west down that shoulder back into Corral Creek, to form a loop hike.

We suggest that all but really experienced hikers simply return to the trailhead—the way you came. You will know you are near the trail going back down into the bowl when you reach the group of evergreen trees. Take the trail going left and angle back down into the middle of the bowl. Go through the woods, this time heading slightly right back onto the Corral Creek Trail, and go back down the ridge.

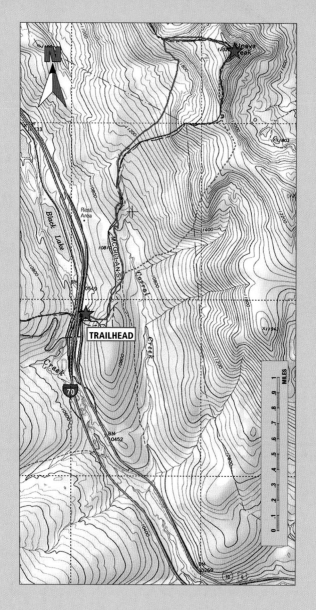

TRAILHEAD

MILES

19. Upper Piney River Trail

BY PAUL RONDEAU

MAPS	Trails Illustrated Vail/Frisco/ Dillon, Number 108 USGS, Vail West & Vail East, 7.5 minute Latitude 40, Vail & Eagle Trails
ELEVATION GAIN	538 feet
RATING	Easy—Lower Valley; Moderate— Falls
ROUND-TRIP DISTANCE	4–6 miles
ROUND-TRIP TIME	2–4 hours
NEAREST LANDMARK	Town of Vail

COMMENT: The Upper Piney River Trail is easily one of the most beautiful places in Colorado, and yet it is only 11 miles from Vail's North Frontage Road. The hike starts near Piney Lake and Piney River Ranch, in the Eagles Nest Wilderness. The trail climbs gradually up the valley, toward what has been called the Maroon Bells of Vail (Peak C and Mount Powell), a breathtaking photo opportunity. The trail meanders its way through a meadow, then aspen and mixed forest, until reaching the beautiful Piney River Falls around the 3.0-mile mark. The trail continues past the falls to Upper Piney Lake, and provides access to a spur trail approaching Mount Powell.

Hiking only the lower valley, containing Piney Lake, offers a great outing for families and less enthusiastic hikers. The open valley is usually prolific with flowers and is relatively flat, climbing less than 100 feet in the first 2 miles.

GETTING THERE: Find Red Sandstone Road, off North Frontage Road—halfway between Vail's two roundabouts (West Vail and Main Vail)—and drive just over 0.5 mile north to the third

The majestic scene of Mount Powell and Peak C, guarding the serene water of Piney Lake.

PHOTO BY FRANK BURZYNSKI

switchback. Here you will turn off (effectively going straight) to the graded gravel road known as Red Sandstone Road No. 700. Although maintained annually, it can get quite "washboardy" and dusty. Be considerate of the many mountain bikers who frequent this ascent into the Gore Range. (Also note the steep drop-off on your left along the way, which is a good thing to be aware of on your way back.)

Drive approximately 10.5 miles on No. 700. The road is sometimes rough, but it is passable for the average automobile. Note there is a multi-year program (started in 2011) to remove beetle-killed lodgepole pine trees, so be alert for large trucks. At the end of the road, park in one of two Forest Service parking lots to your right, just before the gate to a fee area. Known as Piney River Ranch, this pretty area offers canoeing, fishing, horseback riding, and other recreational activities—along with lodging and food service—on its 68 acres.

THE ROUTE: Starting at elevation 9,342 feet, walk a short distance to the trailhead sign (just to the left of the lake) indicating "Public Access, Crossing Private Land—Please stay on the trail." The trail will lead you above and around the Piney River Ranch fee area to the shore of picturesque Piney Lake and the sign "Upper Piney Trail #1885."

Continue on the trail along the lakeshore and upstream toward the upper valley and Piney River Falls (9,880 feet). The trail has several switchbacks through the forested area and a few stream crossings, which are forged on squared-off logs. Eventually you come to the falls hidden in the trees. You will also find many places to rest in the vicinity. Experience Mother Nature at her best, including a rock formation that provides a place to relax, and enjoy the gentle roar of the falls and the light mist that rises from the water below. The area around the falls is home to red columbine and the occasional calypso orchid, among other wildflowers. *Beware*: the many standing pools of water provide a haven for hungry mosquitoes. Retrace your steps back to the trailhead.

Note: The falls are also the breaking-off point to backpack and climb Mount Powell (13,448 feet), the highest peak in the Gore Range. Beyond the falls, the forest transitions to fir and spruce and traverses the river a number of times before reaching a small lake at 5.7 miles. After this point, the climb to Upper Piney Lake (about 8 miles and 1,770 feet from where you started) becomes arduous, and the faint trail can be, at times, difficult to follow. From the lake, at the head of the basin, one can look for the low spot in the ridge to the south; essentially a saddle between the Upper Piney Lake basin and the Booth Lake basin. The "thru-hike" from Piney Lake to Upper Piney, over the saddle, down to Booth Lake, past Booth Falls and, eventually, to the trailhead in East Vail requires a shuttle, and is a long day or multi-day tour of our "backyard." Be prepared and plan accordingly.

Even if you turn around before Piney River Falls, you can still be proud of yourself and tell others about a great outing.

20. Vail Mountain—
Eagle's Loop

BY COLLEEN WIDLAK

MAPS	Vail Mountain Summer Trail Map Latitude 40, Vail & Eagle Trails
ELEVATION GAIN	Minimal
RATING	Easy, wheel chair accessible
ROUND-TRIP DISTANCE	1 mile
ROUND-TRIP TIME	0.5 hour
NEAREST LANDMARK	Eagle Bahn Gondola at Lionshead, Vail

COMMENT: Although 10,350 feet above sea level, Eagle's Loop is the easiest trail in this guidebook. The ski lift affords a unique opportunity for anyone to enjoy an exciting gondola ride while experiencing beautiful alpine vistas.

You can enjoy a variety of games and adventures and an easy hike to Vail's Wedding Deck, with magnificent views along the way. This walk is a treat for the whole family—even those with no hiking experience. With a bit of luck, you may find a snowfield and have a snowball fight right in the middle of summer. You can treat yourself to a bite to eat and your favorite beverage while taking in the extraordinary scenery.

GETTING THERE: From the roundabout in Vail Village, drive west on Frontage Road approximately 0.5 mile to the Lionshead parking lot. Park there and walk toward the mountain and the wheelchair accessible Eagle Bahn Gondola. As you ride up to Eagle's Nest, enjoy the spectacular views of Vail Mountain and the Gore Range. Below, you will see the

One of the many beautiful views from Vail Mountain.
PHOTO BY SCOTT MCCLARRINON

busy hiking and biking trails of the Lionshead area of Vail Mountain.

Note: Unless you already have a season ski pass, the ride on the gondola is currently $30. This includes a $15 credit toward concessions or activities at Adventure Ridge (see below).

THE ROUTE: Upon exiting the Eagle Bahn Gondola Building, take an immediate right, down the ramp. Stop at the Pastor Don and June Simonton Observation Deck, where you can experience the spectacular view of Mount of the Holy Cross. Included in the panorama are Whitney Peak, Middle Mountain, Notch Mountain, Mount Jackson, Grouse Mountain, and Gold Dust Peak. These impressive peaks are all part of the Sawatch Mountain Range.

From the deck you can also see Vail Ski Area's Game Creek Bowl. Turn around to enjoy the Gore Range to the north, hovering over Vail Valley.

Continue west on the paved walkway, up a slight incline, and follow the "Wedding Deck" signs. Keep left on the trail unless there are signs and staff indicating that the path is closed for a private event.

The Wedding Deck is above the Vail Game Creek, known to local skiers as "The Minturn Mile." Wildflowers and even wildlife are abundant along the trail below. From the deck, you can also see Beaver Creek Ski Area and Bachelor Gulch, to the west. After enjoying this beautiful scenery, continue along the loop, which will lead you back to the gondola.

Vail Ski Mountain offers many options for hiking and biking. With the use of the gondola, those wishing to extend their adventure can head out on one of the many trails, while others in the party can ride back down. (Get a copy of the Vail Mountain Summer Trail Map for details.)

One option not listed on the trail map is a long "thru-hike," following Ridge Route Trail to Ptarmigan Loop Trail, to Cougar Ridge Trail, down to Lionshead Rock, and, ultimately, to the town of Minturn. Although it is not listed on the Summer Trail Map, the Cougar Ridge Trail is marked and splits off midway through the Ptarmigan Loop, heading down the ridge toward Minturn.

More notes on your gondola experience: Adventure Ridge offers many activities, including horseback and pony rides, nature hikes, and such lawn sports as bocce, horseshoes, and disc golf. Other options are the Slack Line Park, a climbing wall, and a "Dino Dig" for youngsters. Good eating is available at Talon's Deck Outdoor Grill, Bistro Fourteen, or Game Creek Restaurant.

The gondola is open only Friday through Sunday during the first three weekends of June, from 10 a.m. to 6 p.m. From the last weekend of June through Labor Day, it runs daily from 10 a.m. to 6 p.m., and (usually) through 9 p.m. on Thursday through Sunday. During the remainder of September, the gondola runs only Friday through Sunday, from 10 a.m. through 6 p.m. Check with Mountain Operations for up-to-date information.

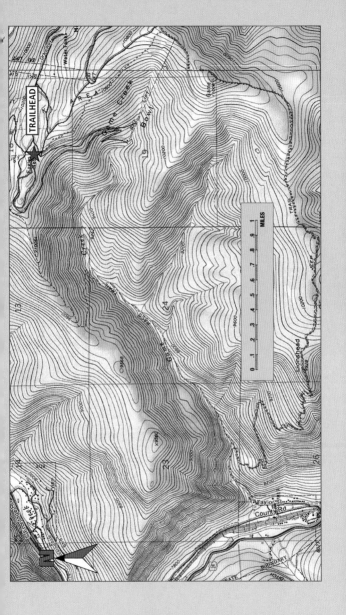

TRAILHEAD

MILES

VAIL MOUNTAIN—EAGLE'S LOOP

Upper Piney River Falls.

About the Author

Nathan Free has spent over 30 years of his life in Colorado—enjoying Mother Nature and the mountains. As a young Boy Scout, he experienced his first 14ers and overnight excursions while gaining a great passion and respect for the outdoors. Over the past 20 years "Nate" has summited all 54/59 peaks over 14,000 feet in Colorado and negotiated hundreds of 13ers, passes, creek explorations, and meadows. Plus, he has hiked all of the trails in this book.

In addition to his hiking, Nate is Scoutmaster for a Vail Boy Scout Troop, a leadership coach, and an enthusiastic bicyclist. He also has been a snow sports instructor for Vail Resorts for 20 years. He shares his world with Lisa Siegert-Free, whose first date with him was on a climb up Snowmass Peak. Lisa continues to support Nate's passion for the outdoors; although her own obsession is linked more to the cute creatures that inhabit those wild places.

Nathan found that writing this book allowed him to revisit some of the wondrous hikes he had enjoyed in earlier years, but had regrettably abandoned in search of new ones. He has found this a great reminder, and metaphor to life—to appreciate what comes to us first.

A cold winter day at the Boston Mining Camp, along the Mayflower
Gulch Trail.

PHOTO BY JUDITH RAU

Checklist

The Best Vail Valley Hikes

☐ HIKE 1	Booth Creek Trail	20
☐ HIKE 2	Bowman's Shortcut to Top of the World	24
☐ HIKE 3	Corral Creek	28
☐ HIKE 4	Gore Valley Trail	32
☐ HIKE 5	Grizzly Creek	36
☐ HIKE 6	Lake Charles/Mystic Island Lake	40
☐ HIKE 7	Lionshead Rock	44
☐ HIKE 8	Lonesome Lake	48
☐ HIKE 9	Mayflower Gulch	52
☐ HIKE 10	Missouri Pass/Fancy Pass	56
☐ HIKE 11	Mount Thomas	60
☐ HIKE 12	New York Mountain	64
☐ HIKE 13	North Trail	68
☐ HIKE 14	Notch Mountain	72
☐ HIKE 15	Seven Sisters Lakes/Fall Creek Pass/ Whitney Peak	76
☐ HIKE 16	Shrine Ridge and Holy Cross Overlook	80
☐ HIKE 17	Tuhare Lakes	84
☐ HIKE 18	Uneva Peak	88
☐ HIKE 19	Upper Piney River Trail	92
☐ HIKE 20	Vail Mountain—Eagle's Loop	96